Qurán

The Universal Message

Guides Mankind to Ways of Peace and Safety

Syed Zahoor Ahmad

authorHOUSE®

AuthorHouse™
1663 Liberty Drive
Bloomington, IN 47403
www.authorhouse.com
Phone: 1 (800) 839-8640

Published by AuthorHouse 11/18/2015

ISBN: 978-1-5049-5820-2 (sc)
ISBN: 978-1-5049-5819-6 (e)

Print information available on the last page.

Any people depicted in stock imagery provided by Thinkstock are models,
and such images are being used for illustrative purposes only.
Certain stock imagery © Thinkstock.

This book is printed on acid-free paper.

Because of the dynamic nature of the Internet, any web addresses or links contained in
this book may have changed since publication and may no longer be valid. The views
expressed in this work are solely those of the author and do not necessarily reflect the
views of the publisher, and the publisher hereby disclaims any responsibility for them.

Acknowledgments

Humeraa Qamar, MPH, MD, FAAP my daughter, and her husband, Asad Qamar, MD, FACC, FCCP, FSGC, FACP, FSCAI for stimulating me into this venture, for providing me with support and an enabling environment in their beautiful home in Ocala, Florida.

My wife Sufia who stood by me all the time with silent encouragement.

Sana, my highly gifted granddaughter, for doing some mundane but essential work for me, despite her many preoccupations while she was a student at Eastside High School, Gainesville, Florida.

Helen Strader, a friend, for typing out the manuscript and proofreading it.

Sam Harris, whose book END OF FAITH provoked me into writing this corrective treatise, as far as Islam, which is my faith, is concerned.

The Ocala Public Library and its staff for providing me with books with smiles and efficiency during research for this book.

Dedicated
to
The Muslims of the World

Prophets Abraham and Ishmail pray:
Our Lord! Make of us Muslims, bowing to your will,
And of our progeny, a people, Muslims, bowing to
Your will. 2:128p

When Jesus found unbelief on their part
He said, "Who will be my helpers in the work of God?"
Said the disciples, "We are God's helpers.
We believe in God
And you bear witness that we are Muslims." 3:52

Don't you see that all beings in the heavens
And on earth bow to God,
Including the sun, the moon, the stars, the trees,
The hills, and the animals. 22:18p

"Only by making an existential surrender (Islam) of his or her whole being
to the basic rhythms of life can a Muslim (one who makes this submission)
live as an authentic human being in the community."

Karen Armstrong, THE BATTLE FOR GOD, Chapter "Muslims:
The Conservative Spirit (1492-1799)

And this (Qurán) is a book which we have revealed as a blessing, so follow it, and be righteous that you may receive mercy.
Qurán 6:155

We send Jesus, son of Mary, with the Gospel: and we ordained in the hearts of those who followed him, compassion and mercy...
Qurán 57:27 p

We gave Moses the book...as a mercy...
Qurán 6:154 p

Contents

An Introductory Note
by
Humeraa Qamar, MD, MPH, FAAP

Read this book and be introduced to an amazing way to approach the **Qurán**. Observations on any subject are scattered throughout the **Qurán**. Gathering them at one place will lead to a fuller and better understanding of the Divine Writ. This is the approach this book has adopted in dealing with the sixteen aspects of the **Qurán**.

Today the Muslim world is in a state of turmoil, strife, and internecine wars. Muslims are murdering Muslims. The Muslim ulemas (clerics,) the Muslim governments, societies, public opinions, and most of all, the Organization of Islamic Countries (OIC) are silent spectators of this tragedy. The Muslim scholars have divided Muslims into sects facing each other as enemies. They are attacking the followers of other faiths and their places of worship, all in violation of the Quranic injunctions.

Your Lord forbids you from killing a human being
Whom God has made sacred;
Except by way of justice and law. 6:151 part

They have divided their religion into sects
Each faction pleased with its own. 30:32

Monasteries, churches, synagogues, and mosques are places where the name of God is commemorated in abundant measure. 22-40 part.

Let me quote more observations of the **Qurán** on illiterate Muslim 'scholars.'

And among them are illiterates who know not the Book
And see therein their own desires
And do nothing but conjecture. 2:78

They are busy spinning tales around Isra (the Prophet's night journey,) Gabriel, heaven and hell, life after death, and the Quranic philosophy of reward and punishment etc. and :

Are "busy" in making a living by repudiating the Qurán.
56:82

And in covering truth with falsehood 2:78

And concealing the truth knowingly. 2:42

For a petty price 2:74

There are some people who vend frivolous tales
To lead astray from the way of God,
Without any knowledge
And take the Book lightly.
There is a degrading punishment awaiting them. 31:6

How could these mullahs be a guide to Muslims? Their knowledge is limited. They are not men of vision. They are unaware of the high issues like war and peace, reward and punishment, history, economics, environment, creation and end of the universes, and of our own abode, the earth, and genesis and evolution of man etc.

In this hopeless situation, who will guide the Muslims? Is there a way out of the Isfallah Safalin (lowest of the low deep) the Muslims have pushed themselves in? Yes, certainly! **Qurán** is the guide, friend, and philosopher of all. The Divine Writ alone is sacred. All other ways are man-made (by Muslim clerics) and need to be consigned to the dustbin. The **Qurán** alone: **Leads you out of darkness, by God's will into**
light

And guides you to the ways of peace and security.

And to a path that is straight. 5:16

These observations relate to mundane issues. We therefore need to concentrate on the affairs of this world as well. What are they? This book mentions the most important ones and need not be repeated here.

We should remind ourselves that the God of Islam is the God of the universes, of all mankind, so is the divine message, so is the Prophet of Islam-a Prophet for all creatures. Muslims are not the favorite of God.

God is full of bounty to mankind. 2:243p

All human beings are equal before God
And all have been gifted the faculty of inspiration. 2:37

And all carry within them a part of the divine spirit. 15:29

The same religion We have sent you by inspiration
With which We inspired Noah, Messengers after him
And on Abraham, Ishmael, Isaac, Jacob,
And the tribes to Jesus, Job, Jonah, Aaron, and Solomon
And to David We give the Psalms. 4:163

The **Qurán** recognizes Buddhism and the Vedic faiths of northern India as well. (See Chapter 5)

God has set a competition between these different ways.

To each among you We have prescribed a Law
And an open way, so strive as in a race in all virtues
And leave it to God to judge you
In matters which you dispute. 5:48p

Everybody will be judged on his or her conduct in this world. The West has adopted the path the **Qurán** prescribes and is flourishing and progressing. Muslims have strayed from the path and are suffering. There is no priesthood in Islam. Muslims are responsible to God and there are no intercessors between them and their creator.

Qurán

This book also deals with the current geopolitical situation in a masterly manner and includes the West's agenda of remaking the world order in their image, the role of the Roman Catholic church and the role of the Muslim fundamentalists, all leading to a clash of civilizations.

This book is strongly recommended to be read by the followers of all faiths to understand Islam, the challenges this faith is facing from within and without, and the current international happenings.

Ocala, Florida

October 2, 2015

In The Name Of God
The Compassionate, The Caring

FOREWORD

The terror plays staged in the United States on 9/11 and re-staged subsequently in many parts of the world have turned out to be significant footprints on the sands of time. The many easterly and westerly winds that have since blown and are continuing to blow with regularity, almost all of them in the Muslim world, instead of obliterating these footprints have given them permanence, like the Ashokan imprints on the rocks.*

The physical structures destroyed on 9/11 are being replaced with loftier buildings. The nightmarish memories of death, agony, and suffering are fading away. But the Pandora's box opened by these events is spreading mischief around the world. The Boston mayhem has caused the world to spin again. What motivated these criminals? This country has given them asylum, peace, self-respect, and opportunities to work out their destinies and their children's. All this is a far cry from the turmoil and insecurity in their mother country from which they fled to Boston, a paradise, only to become fallen men.

Be that as it may, two streams have gushed out of the fallen Two Towers of Manhattan. Both are running parallel to each other and are at loggerheads. Being fed by different perspectives, perceptions, and differing responses and interpretations of the same happenings, they are gathering momentum and may turn into torrents. If unrestrained, they

---

* (Ashoka (304-232 BCE) ruled India as emperor (268-232 BCE.) After a bitterly destructive war with another Indian state, Ashoka, a Hindu, embraced Buddhism and reigned in peace. Edicts of Ashoka, the teachings he wished to be published under his name, were inscribed on rocks throughout his kingdom. A few of these and some other monuments he erected still exist.)

may well bring about tribulation for mankind. Some aver that the seeds of clash of civilizations have been sown. Is the moving finger agitating again? How long before it writes the epilogue?

The first stream is running through the West and is being fed primarily by the West's perceived fear of Muslim terrorism against itself. Islam inspired similar hysteria in the heart of Western Europe in the 16th Century and communism in the entire west in the 20th Century. War on terror is the West's new religion. It has taken the place of the former Cold War. The focus of the United States' might is therefore to destroy Al-Qaeda – its head Osama Bin Laden has been eliminated. Now who is this new Satan? An important military outfit composed of Afghans who formed the overwhelming majority and some Arabs. This was one of the important military groups, the other being Taliban-fighting the Soviet Union who had invaded Afghanistan, a poor and weak neighbor and occupied it. Osama Bin Ladin, to some extent, financed this war effort and wielded considerable influence on Al-Qaeda. The major players, however, were the Pakistani army which was deeply involved in recruiting and training this military machine and Saudi Arabia who provided financial and ideological support to the group. This setting on the world's stage was a gift from the gods for America to weaken and damage their arch rival. It jumped with enthusiasm into the foray with arms and ammunition and dollars to bolster the Afghan resistance. This proved a deadly combination for the Soviet Union. The Russians were soon defeated and retreated, humiliated and disgraced. The heroes of this triumph were no doubt the Al-Qaeda and the Taliban. Even as the Soviet army retreated, it sowed thousands upon thousands of land mines in the Afghan soil, causing innumerable deaths and maiming and blinding thousands of Afghans. It took many months for the United Nations to clear these traps. Even now the land is not totally free of these killers and maimers.

The defeat of the Russians by the Mujahideen opened the door which led to the fragmentation of the USSR and the end of the Cold War. The USSR is no more a super power. The United States occupies the world stage without a peer. In later developments Germany got united. The European Union expanded. The days of centralized Marxist economy came to a sad end. The Western systems of popular democratic governments and free economy where the market forces rule, triumphed. The now Russian Republic reverted to its Byzantine heritage. Most credit for this upheaval which changed the dynamics of international politics, all to the massive benefit of the West, goes to Al-Qaeda and Taliban. They have thus done the greatest favor to the West in post-World War II history.

But, unfortunately and to the regret of the world, once their objective was attained, all three, the Pakistanis, Saudi Arabians, and Americans turned their back on the Afghans, their darling so far. This totally unexpected turn of events left the Mujahideen jobless and fuming in rage. Frustrated and by now aware of their strength and wholly motivated, they turned their guns on the Pakistanis, the Saudis and the Americans.

Now it was the turn of the United States to be taken by surprise. From this day onwards their focus is to fortify their homeland against Al-Qaeda and Osama Bin Laden. In pursuit of these objectives, policies and legislation were hurriedly put in place while the nation was still in shock and panic. These measures were out of all proportion to what was necessary to curb the menace. They are proving more harmful to the United States, without making a dent on terrorism. As a matter of fact, these have fueled it, and extremism is spreading in the world, most of all in the Muslim world, under different names.

Guantanamo Bays have come up in Cuba and elsewhere in the world. The notion of enemy combatants has been set up to bypass the judicial processes. In the name of homeland security, the Executive branch of the government has appropriated more powers to itself. Individual liberties are being circumscribed. The executive is more intrusive of citizens' private lives. In all this, the discerning eyes have noticed internal cracks in the steel armor of justice, equality before law, right to privacy, freedom of speech, and secularism wrapped around this mighty and humane nation's great Constitution-a document which has inspired generations of Americans and nations around the world.

The doctrine of pre-emptive strikes against perceived or imagined threats from enemy nations, has gained currency as an instrument of external policy. Intelligence was doctored to justify invasion of Iraq-a staunch former ally of the West for a long time-and in no way threatened the physical security or economic interest of the United States. The more potent diplomatic approach to ensure energy security and security of Israel and in furtherance of other agendas of the sole super power-some hidden, some obvious- were put on the back burner.

War became the preferred course in the era of President George W. Bush. In this charged atmosphere in the aftermath of 9/11, war against Afghanistan and Iraq became a compulsive urge with the born again Christian. God had sent him on a special mission-to usher in an era of the second wave of Crusades. "This Crusade, this war on terrorism is going to take a while." (George W. Bush, September 16, 2001.) Is this the call of the twenty-first century Pope Urban ll delivered with the Sword of Durendal (see Pg.16-17 for explanation) in his hands?

These costly misadventures have burdened the country with massive indebtedness. This, combined with the inherent weaknesses of the capitalistic system of economy, ("Reckless behavior and unchecked excess is at the heart of the crisis where too many were motivated only by the quick kills and bloated bonuses," President Obama, September 14, 2009) have plunged the Western economy into deep recession bordering on depression. This fiscal crisis has severely affected the stability of the global economy.

The Federal government has doled out multi-trillion dollars in bail outs. State guarantees in some sectors of the economy are no more fake currency. The market economy, a proud pillar of the Western democratic dispensation, has suffered a serious setback. State intervention has come to stay, it appears.

The political dispensation is also crying for reforms. The emergence of new and powerful tools in the political battlefield has altered the dynamics of political science. The print and electronic media, the IT, and tele-messages are all impacting the elections which are now a very costly affair. Donations are a major source of funding. The political parties and their candidates are beholden to the donors. The lobbies and special interest groups are also factors to reckon with. Increasingly today's democracies are being controlled by the rich. They are manipulating the political and economic systems to their own advantage. The income in-equality has emerged as a major concern around the world.

Oxfam, a worldwide charity organization reports that the economic inequality has run out of control. The 85 richest people on the planet own the wealth of half the world's population. The report exposes the pernicious impact of growing inequality that helps the richest undermine democratic processes and drives policies that promote their interests at the expense of everyone else.

Even foreign governments set up watch towers around the time of the presidential elections. So it is time for reform. The influence of all these factors, in my opinion, can be reduced to a great extent by fixing the Presidential term to eight or ten years with no second term option. The term of all elected officials also needs to be extended. This will ensure a sustained attention by the President to vital national and international issues without having to worry about the second term. There will be time enough for the President to see through his agenda and witness its outcome. As it stands, the system is subject to many vagaries.

Historically what Paul Kennedy calls "imperial overstretch," military adventures and the resulting slackening of moral standards and weakening of the economy, have been the major causes of the decline and fall of civilizations. The sole superpower in today's world must rein in its ambitions, arrogance, and disdain of the United Nations and other international agencies. Deference should be shown to public opinion within the country and without. It must re-take the high moral ground of justice and morality in international affairs. This will enable it to regain its status as an honorable and trustworthy state and as an arbiter of last resort in international disputes. At the same time, the United States must recognize its dependence on the rest of the world. Small or large, all countries have their usefulness and demand respect and recognition. Here I am reminded of a story that I had read in middle school.

A mouse in his foolishness once went too close to a lion who was basking in the sun. Annoyed, the lion held the mouse in his paw and told him that death awaited him as a penalty for ignoring to show proper respect to him. The mouse apologized profusely and told the lion that he was the king of the jungle, whereas the mouse was an insignificant denizen of his kingdom. However weak he may be, he could be of some use to the mighty king if the occasion arose. Pleased and flattered, the lion freed the mouse. A few days later the same mouse saw the same lion enmeshed in a net lain by a big game hunter, helpless and facing the prospect of life imprisonment. The mouse ran to his tribe and returned with hundreds of mice. They shredded the net in no time and freed the lion. It was now the turn of the chastened lion to acknowledge and thank his insignificant benefactors.

None is self-sufficient. Super powers are not free from limitations either. There are many uncertainties in the equation of human affairs which are diverse, complex, and unpredictable. As the sole super power of the world, **Do not strut on its stage with insolence. You cannot rend the earth, nor can you reach the mountains in height. Qurán 17:37** Shun arrogance **God does not love the arrogant. 16:22** The lessons of Viet Nam, Iraq, and Afghanistan must always inform and guide US affairs in international conduct.

Equally importantly, the United States must retain its secular character and allow other civilizations to exist, develop, and flourish-the world is large enough for that. Better to avoid meddling with other civilizations and philosophies of life, however, irrational they may look. You cannot re-make the world in your own image. It is good to take to heart one of the recommendations, as a matter of fact, the only sensible recommendation, of Samuel P. Huntington, a proponent of re-making of the world order which favors the white race. "And most important to recognize that Western intervention in the affairs of other civilizations is probably the most dangerous source of instability and potential global conflict in a multi-civilizational world."(THE CLASH OF CIVILIZATIONS AND RE-MAKING OF THE WORLD ORDER) In any case, the claim of the West that its political and economic systems are the best of all alternative systems and their mission to make them universal is no more valid. So why go to war in their name?

All this may look like stating the obvious, or is it re-stating the obvious which mankind may ignore to its peril?

Whatever their failing, I am however sure of one thing. The United States is God's chosen nation at this point of time in history; chosen for the fulfillment of God's plan. Mankind therefore has a stake in the continuous development and prosperity of the US. The generosity and humaneness of the US and its citizens have touched the world. All countries have benefitted from them. They look up to the US for help and succor in times of distress and are never disappointed. At the same time, the world blames the US for any catastrophe that may happen anywhere in the world-the price of being a super power. And yet all the blamers aspire to being citizens of the US! The US civilization is by far the greatest civilization mankind has ever seen. This country's relentless pursuit of knowledge, technology, and research in IT, genetics, all branches of sciences, cosmology, missile technology, medicine, nanosciences, and myriad new branches of knowledge are mind boggling. Take 2012 for example, the sequencing of the human genome, the creation of the encyclopedia of DNA elements known as encode, the landing of the Curiosity rover on Mars after eighteen months and three hundred and fifty million mile journey through space (the sun is only ninety million miles away from our planet) are some of the peaks of human achievement.

In January, 2013, NASA released for publication an amazing colored image of the Large Magellanic Cloud, a satellite galaxy of the Milky Way, two-hundred thousand light years away from Earth! Do you know how distant is that? Light travels at the rate of one hundred and eighty-six thousand miles per second. Multiply this with sixty and sixty and twenty-four and three hundred and sixty-five to determine the distance light travels in one light year. Multiply this with two hundred and eighty thousand. This is the distance NASA computers have probed and sent back this spectacular colored image. The write-up further says that as the Milky Way's gravity tugs on its neighbors' gas clouds, they collapse to form new stars! Let us state what the **Qurán** has to say on this:

Every day God manifests Himself in yet wondrous ways. Which one of your sustainers' powers will you deny?
55:29p, 30

All this is beyond the comprehension of the vast majority of the humans. Its significance and impact on human life in the future is accessible only to a miniscule part of the privileged humans endowed with mighty intellect, knowledge, faith, wisdom, and most of all, inspiration.

But no one knows its explanation but God and those deeply rooted in knowledge and none will grasp the message except men of understanding. 3:7p

And men who remember God standing, sitting, and lying down on their sides and contemplate the wonders of creation in the heavens and earth. 3:191p

In whose hearts God has inscribed faith and whom he has strengthened with inspiration from Himself 58:22 (For full details see Chapters 1-2 and 4.)

In its generosity, social justice, justice according to law, respect for various faiths and beliefs, human dignity and its striving after knowledge and its secular character, the US, I believe, is closest to the Islamic polity as laid down in the **Qurán**, more so than any Muslim country.

Social Justice in *Islamic Polity*

God tells the prophet: **They ask you how much are they to spend in charity? Say, "What is beyond your needs." 2:219 p**

Did He not find you an orphan and take care of you? Did He not find you poor and enrich you? So do not oppress the orphan and do no rebuff the seeker. 93:8-10

It is not righteous that you turn your faces towards East or West. But it is righteousness to spend of your substance out of love for God, on your kin, on orphans, on the needy, the wayfarer, on those who ask, and for the ransom of slaves.

2:177 p

There is a recognized right in your wealth for the needy. 70:24,25p

Any charity you give is a beautiful loan to God and you will be paid back a thousand times. 73:20p (For full details, see Chapter 5)

Justice According to Law and Respect for Human Life

God is the best of judges. 6:57p

God commands you to render back your trusts to whom they are due. And when you judge between man and man judge with justice. 4:58p

Believers stand out firmly for justice as witnesses to God, even if it be against yourselves, or your parents, or relatives, whether one

be rich or poor. God is closer and more worthy than either. And do not follow desires lest you swerve from justice and if you pervert it or neglect it, God is aware of what you do. 4:135

Do not take life which God has made sacred except by way of justice and law. You are thus commanded so that you learn wisdom. 6:151p

For those who defy right and justice,
There is a grievous penalty. 42:42p

Verily justice must come to pass. 51:6p

God loves those who are just. 60:8p

And do not take life which God has made sacred except in a just cause. If anyone is killed wrongfully We have given to his heir authority to demand blood money or to forgive. But he should not exceed the limits of justice by slaying the killer, for he will be judged by the same law. 17:33

You see, Islam discourages the penalty of death for death.

See Chapter 10 for details.

Qura'nic Views on Other Religions and Faiths and its Secular Character

The same religion We have sent you by inspiration which we enjoined on Abraham, Moses, and Jesus. 42:13p

Say, "We believe in God and the revelation given to us and to Abraham, Ishmael, Isaac, Jacob and the tribes and that given to Moses and Jesus and given to all prophets from their Lord. We make no distinction between any of them." 2:136

The Muslims, the Jews, the Christians, and the Sabians, have their reward with their Lord. There is nothing for them to fear, nor shall they grieve. 2:62p

To each among them we have established a law and a revealed way. So let your goals be everything good. Your destiny and everyone's, is to God. 5:48p

And this Qurán is a book which We have revealed as a blessing, so follow it that you may receive mercy. 6:155

We sent Jesus, son of Mary, with the Gospel, and we ordained in the hearts of those who followed him compassion and mercy. 57:27p

We gave Moses the Book as a mercy. 6:154p (For full details see Chapter 5.)

Knowledge

Among the first revelation, if not the first, received by Prophet Muhammad is: **Recite in the name of your Lord who created-from an embryo, created the human. Recite "Your Lord is all-giving Who taught by the pen-taught the human what he did not know before." 96:1-5**

In these five verses, "recite," "taught," "pen," "know," all instruments and mediums of learning have been mentioned six times, underlying the supreme importance Islam attaches to knowledge. **Qurán** means recitation. **This Book is not for the illiterates. 27:8p**

No one knows the Qurán's explanation but God and those deeply rooted in knowledge. 3:7p

And who are the men deeply rooted in knowledge? They are those who are engaged in expanding the frontiers of knowledge, who are able to probe into the mysteries behind the visible and the invisible phenomenon of nature.

The keys of the unseen are with God and God knows what is on the earth and in the sea and not a leaf falls but God knows it …all is inscribed in a record to those who can read. 6:59p

All the celestial bodies swim along, each in its rounded course. The sun and the moon follow courses exactly compounded. Each just swims along in its orbit according to law.

Verily in this are signs for men who are wise. 221:31, 55:5, 36:40p, 16:12p

Verses relating to knowledge have been put together in Chapter 4.

Secular Dimension

Say, "Atheists, I do not worship what you worship, nor do you worship what I worship. You have your way and I have my way." 109:2-3, 6

Monasteries, churches, synagogues, and mosques-in them the name of God is commemorated in abundant measure. 22:40p

It is therefore vital for Muslims living in the US to be loyal to the country, to respect it, and take full advantage of the tremendous opportunities it has to offer in all fields of human endeavor. This is an opportunity to pay back to some extent, if not fully, the debt we all owe this country. Muslims must look up to US as a model to follow-opposing it will only end up in their destruction. After all, the West is where it is today because of its encounter with the Islamic civilization in the Middle Ages. It is now our turn to receive back what we gave Europe in the Middle Ages. (800-1400 CE) Europe owes its Renaissance and Reformation to Islam.

And 9/11. What is the reality behind 9/11? I am reminded of a murderous but failed attack on Pope Paul John XI by a Turkish Muslim. The world quickly knew that he was a hired assassin, not a terrorist. As soon as 9/11 happened, some worrying and dissenting voices at variance with the known and accepted version were heard. I do not want to go into details. It may be a long time before we know all the facts.

The Second Stream-The Al-Qaeda Perspective

All what has been said so far has been noted and absorbed by Al Qaeda and their allies. For them the modern conflict with the West had its genesis in the fall of the Shah of Iran in 1979. The unsettled conditions in Iran and the American preoccupation with it stirred once again in the USSR the centuries old Russian imperial dream of access to the warm waters of the Indian Ocean through Afghanistan and the now Pakistani province of Baluchistan. Reassured of the American indifference, the Soviet Union as a first step invaded and occupied Afghanistan, a poor and weak neighbor. The twelve years or so of brutal military rule and savagery of the occupied forces, surpassing in intensity Stalin's savagery against its central Asian Muslim population, totally devastated Afghanistan. The whole population was traumatized. Millions of Afghans were killed or maimed. Afghan cities, infrastructure, and irrigation systems were severely battered. The aim was to turn Afghanistan into a communist satellite state like Poland and other eastern European countries bordering the Soviet Union.

Now what is this? Not terrorism of the most brutal type, ask the Afghans. Then again intelligence was doctored to justify the U.S.'s second attack on Iraq, devastating the country. You do not call this terrorism? How about the first US attack on Iraq? The Al Qaeda classifies the two attacks as pure terrorism. How about the Israeli attack and destruction of a nuclear facility under construction in Baghdad?

A combination of the finest fighting forces (NATO, US) attacked their former favorite allies. The Afghan Mujahideen, dressed in rags and bare feet, have for all purposes, defeated the Western forces.

An attempt by the Serbs to exterminate Bosnian Muslims was defeated by the United States' direct military intervention. Europe otherwise was a silent spectator to this genocide.

Then there is the festering Israeli-Palestinian conflict.

The man-made global warming causing heightened tsunamis, rising sea levels, shrinking natural resources and seafood, droughts in some areas of the world, and excessive rain in some others has endangered the human species. This ecological imbalance is the result of the reckless use of natural resources by the West. Is this not terrorism against humanity?

Worldwide economic recession, again caused by the West; is this not economic terrorism?

Such is the perspective from which the Jihadists are drawing strength and inspiration. Their response has terrified the world. Because of them, a small marginalized brain-washed group of Muslims, the world today is a more dangerous place to live than at any other time in history. The worrying factor is that Wahabism, (see pg.30) which is providing ideological support to the Jihadists, is rapidly spreading among the Muslims the world over. Mainstream Muslims are the greatest sufferers of their activities. Muslims are killing Muslims. A small but rapidly expanding minority is attempting to drag them into dark ages. They have degraded Islam, the message of the Prophet. They have pulled down the Divine to their level, instead of struggling to ascend up to Him which is their destiny.

Forever toiling towards your Lord,
Painfully toiling, but you shall meet Him. 84:6
To each among them we have established a law and a revealed way.
So let your goals be everything good. Your destiny and everyone's,
is to God. 5:48p

Their activities are rapidly isolating the mainstream Muslims from other civilizations. They have set themselves up against the West and other faiths, creeds, etc. This stream which is spreading like a scourge in the Muslim world is causing untold damage to the Muslim community. Islam is under siege in the hands of its followers. Their emphasis is on rituals which have lost their spiritual content. Their purpose is to show their neighbors how holy they are. The **Qurán** is aware of such happenings and warns Muslims thus.

Do you see the one who rejects religion? That is the one who rebuffs
the orphan and does not encourage feeding the poor. So woe to
those who pray and yet are inattentive to their prayers. Those who
want to be seen by men and yet refuse neighborly needs. 107:1-7

Their source of inspiration is the Shariah-a man-made body of secondary laws, framed more than a thousand years ago and still in practice. There are as many Shariahs as there are sects and sub-sects, all claiming authenticity for themselves and facing each other as deadly opponents. They have relegated the **Qurán**-the Divine message- to a tertiary position. These man made laws concentrate on issues of little significance. The **Qurán** anticipates this situation.

But there are some people among the Muslims who vend amusing
tales
To lead astray from the way of God and making a joke of it.
There is a degrading punishment in store for them. 31:6

They have divided their religion into sects,
Each faction pleased with its own. 30:32

And do not sell My signs for a petty price; and do not cover truth with falsehood and do not conceal truth knowingly. 24:2p-24:3p

As for those who conceal the evidences and the guidance
We have sent down, after We made them clear to humanity in the Book,
God curses them, and those who curse curse them. 2:159

It is time they repent and relent.

This stream, if allowed to develop, also portends disaster for mankind. How do we stop them? By bringing, I believe, onto the main stage the Islam based on the Divine message. The battle needs to be fought out primarily in the ideological battleground. Military action against them is and will continue to be of little avail. Enlightened Muslim scholars should go on television and the print media. This book is one such humble attempt.

9/11 has resurfaced the anti-Muslim outburst in the West which has been a recurring feature in history which began when the Roman church decided to recapture Jerusalem from Muslim occupation in the closing years of the eleventh century. The ground was prepared by the Catholic Church by creating anti-Muslim hysteria in Western Europe. Lies and more lies were invented and harnessed to create hatred of Muslims. The "Song of Roland" was the best example.

At the end of Charlemagne's campaign in Spain in 778 CE, the Franks had been crossing the Pyrenees on their homeward march when the rear guard got separated from the main army. It was ambushed and massacred by an army of Basques, a local Christian community. Among the slain was Roland, Duke of the Marches and Brittany, and the hero of the in famous "Song of Roland." In the poem, however, the people who attacked Roland are Muslims, not Basques. Roland's most valued possession was his sword, Durendal, a weapon of supernatural powers. With this sword Roland killed hundreds of Muslims before he was murdered. The poet dwells on this slaughter in delighted but gruesome detail. (Reference: Karen Armstrong-HOLY WAR-THE CRUSADES AND THEIR IMPACT ON TODAY'S WORLD – Chapter-"Before the Crusades")

For Pope Urban II, Charlemagne and "Song of Roland" provided the inspiration when he summoned the first crusade. Such falsification of history is still going on. Pope Benedict XVI, a German, delivered a lecture at the University of Regensburg, Germany, on September 20, 2006. The talk was primarily an attack on Islam. Setting aside the wedge between the Christian churches of the Greek East and Latin West, the Pope quoted with approval a fourteenth century obscure Byzantine emperor, Manual II who was reported to have said, "Show me just what Mohammad brought that was new and they will find things only evil and inhuman, such as his command to spread by the sword the faith he preached." In the fourteenth century the Eastern part of the Byzantine Empire had been overrun by Muslims and Constantinople, its capital, the second Rome was under threat. Such ravings against the Prophet of his triumphant enemy was understandable, though belied by history. Talking to Newsweek, the renowned US weekly on this issue, William A. Graham, the dean of the Harvard Divinity School stated that "Islam spread far more thoroughly by proselytizing than by the sword."

Arnold J. Toynbee, the renowned historian and a Nobel laureate has this to say: "On the eve of the second and final fall of Constantinople in 1453, the medieval Greek Orthodox Christians …would rather behold in Constantinople the turban of Muhammad than the Pope's Tiara or a cardinal's hat." Reference CIVILIZATION ON TRIAL, chapter "Russia's Byzantine Heritage."

This shocking falsification of history is still in vogue with the Roman church. The Pope, the 265th Vicar of Christ on earth, occupying the throne of St. Peter, the chief shepherd of the 1.1 billion Roman Catholic community and their supreme pontiff, quite conveniently forgot to mention his church's infamous role in the massacre of the Jews in Hitler's Germany. He also conveniently forgot what the Vatican Ecumenical Council declared in 1962: "That Islam has given mankind important truths about God, Jesus and the prophets." Thus the Roman Church is quick to harness the post 9/11 anti-Muslim hype for its own purposes.

Whatever their failings, for Muslims speaking ill of prophets of other religions or their scriptures is blasphemy. Why?

Abraham the chosen one here in the world and one of the best in the world to come. 21:30p

Abraham the true in faith-a friend of God. 4:125p

God held mystic conversation with Moses on Mount Sinai. 19:52

God gave Moses the book…as a mercy. 6:154p

God strengthened Jesus with the Holy Spirit. 2:87p

God taught Jesus the book, and wisdom, the Law and the Gospel. 51:10p (for full details see chapter 5)

A section of the Muslims believe that the present (2013) unrest noticeable in the Muslim world is an engineered affair. True or not, this is entirely according to the wishes of the Catholic Church and Al-Qaeda. Both are gleefully casting their fishing nets in troubled waters in the Muslim world. The Church, it seems, has unlimited funds at its disposal for this purpose.

Such are the tributaries feeding the second stream. If unchecked, it has the potential to create mischief-great mischief on God's earth. As the West has experienced, war against Al-Qaeda and the Taliban boomerangs. They are soldiers with faith defending their homeland, fighting for a holy cause. Life for them has no value. The West must recognize that this spiritual weapon in their armory is not easily overcome. Let me quote Arnold J. Toynbee on this. Citing historical precedents, he observes: "Today in the 21st century, the West is again the victim of similar hysteria inspired by Islam." This is in spite of the fact. "The concentric attack of the modern West upon the Islamic world has inaugurated the present encounters between the two civilizations. This is seen as part of the still large and ambitious movement in which the Western civilization is aiming at nothing less than the incorporation of all mankind in a single great society and the total control of all resources of earth, air, and sea by means of modern Western technology… Thus the contemporary encounter between Islam and the West is more active and intimate. It is also distinctive in being an incident by Western man to Westernize the world… Thus Islam is once more facing the West with her back to the wall, but this time the odds are heavily against her because the modern West is superior to her, not only in arms, but also in the technique of economic life on which military science ultimately depends." Then why all this hysteria in the today's West? Toynbee's reply is: "Islam's creative gift is monotheism…Islam though down and out is fully capable of rising from the ashes and confronting the West once again…Under the impact of the West, the great deeps of Islam are already stirring." Reference Toynbee's CIVILIZATION ON TRIAL, Chapter 10, "Islam, the West, and the future."

Another by-product of 9/II is that the book market is flooded with anti-Islamic literature, full of half-truths and falsehoods. Most of the writers have misread Islam, have misquoted the **Qurán**, and are maligning the Prophet of Islam in their attempt to link terrorism to the Qura'nic teachings and the conduct of the Prophet of Islam. Their purpose was to make quick bucks by pandering to the popular sentiments against the Muslims. Whatever their intentions, they have certainly succeeded in poisoning the gullible man in the street. My concern however is with books claiming to be scholarly and yet misrepresenting Islam. These are the books that have led me to venture into writing this book. Let me quote a few examples from my recent readings.

Michael Cook, in his book THE KORAN, A VERY SHORT INTRODUCTION published by the Oxford University Press quotes the following verse from the **Qurán** in support of a point of view he is discussing: **"There is nothing but our present life, we die and we live and nothing but Time (dahr) can destroy us." 45:24**

Now let me reproduce the full text of this verse.

And they say: "What is there but our life in this world?
We shall die and we live, and nothing but Time (dahr)
Can destroy us. But of that they have no Knowledge.
They merely conjecture." 45:24

See the difference? By conveniently leaving out the last sentence of the verse, the meaning has been reversed.

Mr. Sam Harris in his book THE END OF FAITH, Chapter 4, contends that Judaism, Christianity, and Islam are evil, that their repository is the trash can. My concern here is about Islam, my faith. Before I take up this issue, let me discuss an interesting observation of Sam Harris which applies to all three religions. "There is no telling what our world would now be like had some great Kingdom of Reason emerged at the time of Crusades and pacified the credulous multitudes of Europe and Middle East. We might have had modern democracy and the Internet by the year 1600."

Excellent pearls of wisdom. I may be permitted to pose a counter question. If the Fairy Queen had in her infinite concern for man waved her wand and directed the great kingdom of reason to pacify the senseless rulers involved in internecine European wars, the two devastating World Wars (not forgetting Nagasaki and Hiroshima) and the Cold War that followed in their wake, and if the Fairy Queen had further directed that the limitless potential of the nuclear energy be harnessed in the service of mankind only, and not to destroy it, what would the world be like today? (2013) It would be a paradise without wars, without hunger, ignorance, disease, superstition and poverty. It would be an Arcadia, an Utopia, in fulfillment of man's innermost urgings through the ages. Do we hold religion responsible for this?

Reverting to Sam Harris' ravings about Islam in the chapter "The Problem with Islam," he contends that "Islam is a religion of conflict. On almost every page the **Qurán** prepares the ground for religious conflict, on almost every page the book instructs observant Muslims to despise non-believers, that Islam's God is a warlord, and the outer Jihads is a war against infidels or apostates is a central feature of the faith." He further contends that "the basic thrust of Islamic doctrine is undeniable-convert, subjugate or kill unbelievers, kill apostates and conquer the world!" These atrocious utterances made me believe that Harris has never read the **Qurán**. He is unaware of the Qura'nic concepts of God, believers, heaven, hell, apostasy, its philosophy of reward and punishment, man's destiny, etc. In support of his contention he has selected sixty verses, most of them partial, out of six thousand plus verses the **Qurán** consists of. Those born as Christians or Jews, believing or not, practicing or not, tend to equate the Islamic God with their own Gods. Is this so? Find the answer in Chapter 2 of this book.

Now to Sam's quotes on Islam, I will take up the very first verse:

**It is the same to them whether you warn them
Or do not warn them; the un-believers will have no faith. 2:6**

Who are the unbelievers? Let me quote the relevant Qura'nic verses in full:

**This is the Book, in it is guidance without doubt, for the conscientious
Those who believe in the unseen who practice regular prayer,
And who give of what we have provided them**

And those who believe in what was revealed to you
And what was revealed before your time. And who are certain of
the Hereafter.
They follow guidance from their Lord; and they are the successful
ones.
As for those who disbelieve it is the same to them
Whether you warn them or not-they will not believe. 2:2-6

The **Qurán** defines a believer as one who:

1. Fears God
2. Believes in the existence of that which is beyond human perception
3. Is constant in prayers
4. Spend on others out of what God has provided him
5. Believes in what was revealed to Muhammad (P. B. U. H) and
   revealed before his time
6. And has the assurance of the hereafter.

Say: "We believe in God, and in what has been revealed to us

And what was revealed to Abraham, Ishmael, Isaac, Jacob, and
the Tribes,
And in the books given to Moses and Jesus, and that given to all
the Prophets, From their Lord: we make no distinction between
one and another among them
And to God we submit." 2:136

We revealed the Book to you in truth, confirming the scriptures
that came before it. For each of them we have established a law,
and a revealed way. If God had so willed, He would have made you
a single nation-but the intent is to test you in what God has given
you. So strive as in a race in all virtues. The goal of you all is to God,
Who will tell you about that wherein you differed. 5:48p

Believers, believe in God and God's messenger, and the Book
That God has sent down to the messenger,
And whoever repudiates God and God's angels, Books, and
messengers,
And the last day has already gone far astray. 4:136

These are the signs of the Book full of wisdom,
Guidance and mercy for those who do good,
And who are certain of the hereafter; and they are the ones who thrive. 31:2-5

The **Qurán** claims that many nations, races, and tribes are recipients of God's messages conveyed through prophets born into them and names twenty-five prophets. Noah, (P.B.U.H) Abraham, (P.B.U.H) Moses, (P.B.U.H) Jesus, (P.B.U.H) and Muhammad (P.B.U.H) get extensive mention in the **Qurán**. This is one of the fundamental doctrines of the **Qurán**: the doctrine of the historical continuity of divine revelation with more or less the same core message. For full detail I'll refer the reader to Chapter 5, "Islam and Other Religions."

Say: "Come, I will rehearse what God has prohibited you from;… join not

Anything as equal with Him; be good to your parents; kill not your children

On a plea of want-We provide sustenance for you and for them-come not

Nigh to shameful deeds, whether open or secret; take not life, which God Has made sacred, except by way of justice and law;

Thus does He command you, that you may learn wisdom."
6:151

People of the Book! There has come to you our messenger, revealing to you much that you used to hide in the Book.
And passing over much by which God guides those
Who follow divine will to the ways of peace and safety
And brings them from darkness into light, by divine leave,
And guides them to a straight path.   5:15-16

The Muslims, the Jews, the Christians, and the Sabians,
And any who believe in God and the last day and do good

Have their reward with their Lord. There is nothing for them to fear; They will not sorrow. 2:62

As for the Muslims, the Jews, the Sabians˙, the Christians, the Magians, and the polytheists God will decide among them on the day of resurrection, for God is witness to all things. 22:17

Monasteries, churches, and synagogues and mosques are places wherein the name of God is commemorated in abundant measure. 22:40p

The following verses of the **Qurán** however are significant and need to be remembered at all times:

Among the people of the Book is a community that is upstanding. They read the signs of God through the hours of night,

Prostrating themselves. They believe in God and the last day And enjoin what is right and forbid what is repugnant. And race to good deeds. They are among the righteous. And whatever good they do, they will not be denied it. God knows the conscientious.   3:113-115

These are no isolated verses. By the time you have finished reading this book, you will come to know that this is the burden of the **Qurán**. Seen in perspective, the confusion and more importantly the misunderstanding, sought to be created by quoting out of context, or partial quoting of some verses of the **Qurán** falls though.

I will take up one more example to reinforce my submission. Sam Harris cites four verses (**2:190-193**) in proof of his contention that Islam's God is a warlord. These are also the favorite verses with some

---

˙ The Sabians seem to have been a monotheistic religious group intermediate with Judaism and Christianity. Their name probably derived from the Arabic verb tsebha: "He immersed himself (in water)" would indicate that they were followers of John the Baptist-in which case, they could be identified with the Mandaleans, a community that to this day is to be found in Iraq. (Ref. THE MESSAGE OF THE QURA'N by Muhammad Asad) See also Encyclopedia Britannica under the heading "Sabians."

Western writers who have approached the **Qurán** with jaundiced eyes in search of some basis for their hostile notions on Islamic Jihad.

Slay them wherever you find them, idolatry is worse than carnage.

If they attack you, put them to the sword. Thus shall the unbelievers be rewarded; but if they desist God is forgiving and merciful. Fight against them until idolatry is no more and God's religion reigns supreme. But if they desist, fight none except the evildoers. 2:190,193

I will now quote these verses in full.

Fight in God's cause against those who wage war against you, but do not commit aggression-for verily God does not love aggressors. And slay them wherever you come upon them, and drive them away from wherever they drove you away-for oppression is even worse than killing. And fight them not at the sacred mosque (The sacred mosque refers to the mosque in Mecca)**unless they first fight against you but if they fight you, slay them; such shall be the recompense of those who deny the truth. But if they desist behold God is much forgiving and dispenser of grace. Hence fight against them until there is no more oppression and worship is devoted to God alone. 2:190-2:193** God here is inclusive of Gods of Judaism and Christianity.

Thus Islam does not sanctify aggression, it permits war only in self-defense and war against oppression and in defense of decent values. Islam condemns killing and aggression; but once the war is on, it follows its own logic (and slay them wherever you come upon them.) Please note that even this war in self-defense and against oppression is oriented against the Arab pagans in Mecca.

Even here, the emphasis is on terminating the state of war at the earliest and to restore normalcy and peace. Islam abhors violence and killing without due process of law, holds life sacred, and exhorts mankind to avoid mischief on God's earth. Reference **6:151**and **7:56** Muhammad (P.B.U.H) has been sent **as a mercy to all creatures. 21:107As a witness, a bearer of glad tidings, and a warner.33:45 And as one who invites to God's grace by His leave and as a lamp spreading light 33:46 We created not the heavens, the earth, and all**

between them, but for just ends. The hour is surely coming when all this will be manifest. So overlook any human faults with gracious forgiveness. 15:85

To each is a goal to which God turns him: then strive together towards all that is good. Wherever you are God will bring you together. God has power over all things. 2:148

The **Qurán** reinforces this vital aspect. **Say, "I will rehearse what God has prohibited you from. Do not join anything with Him. Be good to your parents. Do not kill your children on a plea of want. Do not commit any shameful deeds, be they open or secret and do not take any human being's life, the life which God has declared to be sacred, otherwise than in pursuit of justice." Thus God enjoins upon you so that you may learn wisdom. 6:151**

Mercy and forgiveness are the overwhelming attributes of God. Every Muslim remembers God with: "In the name of God, the compassionate, the merciful" dozens of times a day. God is most forgiving, most merciful, is mentioned in the **Qurán** in a hundred places.

There is an evolution in the Qura'nic aspect of God from a personal being at the base, to the Light, the ultimate Reality and the Truth at the apex. He is universal, God of all mankind and created beings. His bounty, mercy, and forgiveness extend to all humans. For a comprehensive discussion please refer to Chapter 2, "The Divine Defined"

Qurán is a book of guidance, a source of mercy and blessing and healing, like the Old Testament and the New Testament as revealed to Moses and Jesus.

And Islam's doctrine to convert, subjugate, kill non-believers, kill apostates, and conquer the world? In making this statement, Mr. Harris has strayed far, far away from Islam. Muhammad was not sent to dispose of the affairs of others, nor as a guard over them. His only responsibility was to communicate the message. There is no compulsion in religion. All faiths have truths in them. Every nation has been given a way and a law and it is expected that it will live accordingly. If Islam appeals to reason, accept it, or go your way.

Kill Apostates, Unbelievers

And if any of you turn back from their faith their acts will be fruitless in this world and in the hereafter. 2:217p God does not guide those who reject faith after they have accepted it. The curse of God, His angels, and all mankind is on them.3:86-7p The unbelievers have already been defined earlier.

Once Mr. Sam Harris is clear on the definition of God, and the message of the **Qurán**, his assertion about unbelievers and apostates, and his claim that Islam is evil crashes like a house of cards before a storm.

At one point, Sam Harris states: "To convey the restlessness with which the unbelievers are vilified in the text of the Koran, I provide a long compilation of quotations below in order of their appearance in the text. This is what the creator of the universe apparently has on his mind when he's not fussing with gravitational constants and atomic weights."

The **Qurán** has more than six thousand verses; out of these about a thousand emphasize the supreme importance of knowledge and exhorts mankind to learn and acquire knowledge. One of the most potent prayers in the **Qurán is Oh God, increase my knowledge.** More of this in Chapters 2 and 4. At this point, I will quote a few passages from the **Qurán** in answer to Sam's sarcastic insinuation about the Creator of the Universe.

Do not the unbelievers see that the heavens and the earth were joined together as one unit before we clove them asunder? We made from water every living thing. 21:30

It is He Who created the night and the day, the sun and the moon: all the celestial bodies, each floating in its rounded course. 21:33

(Remember Galileo (1564-1642) who made the same assertion a thousand years later and was punished by the Roman church?)

He who created the seven heavens one above another, no want of proportion will you see in the creation of the most Gracious. So turn your vision again: do you see any flaw? Then look twice again and your vision will come back to you weak and weary. 67:4

The sun and the moon follow courses exactly compounded. 55:5

God has raised high the firmament and has set up the balance of justice in order that you may not transgress due balance. 56:8

It is not permitted to the sun to catch up the moon, nor can the night outstrip the day, each just swims along in its own orbit according to law. 36:40

Do they not look at the birds held poised, in the air, in the sky. There are signs here for people who understand. 16:79

The sun and the moon,
each runs for a determined period. 13:2p

Glorify the name of your Guardian-Lord Who has created and further given order and proportion; Who has ordained laws and granted guidance. 87:1-3

Do no mischief on the earth after it has been set in order. 7:56
(another reminder of THE INCONVIENENT TRUTH, Al Gore.)

We have not created the heavens and the earth and all that is in between them but in due proportion and for a definite term. 46:3p

We created not the heavens, the earth and all between them but for just ends. And the hour is surely coming when this will be manifest. So overlook any human faults with gracious forgiveness. 15:85

(Full details can be found in Chapters 2 and 4.)

Please be assured that the Qura'nic God as the Creator of the universe is fully aware of the laws governing the universe of His making, as well as the well-being and concerns of humankind. All the rubbish Sam Harris ascribes to God and the **Qurán** is no more than his un-informed opinion reflecting his dislike of all organized religions.

Even some discerning Western scholars have at times, (but infrequently) misunderstood or inadvertently misinterpreted the **Qurán**. Jonathan Bloom and Sheila Blair for example, in their commendable book A THOUSAND YEARS OF FAITH AND POWER have this to state: "Narrative elements in the Koran are the easiest to remember, but in contrast to the Bible, they actually form a very small part of the whole. Most of the narratives are versions of traditional stories found in other near Eastern cultures. For example, God's creations of the world in six days and his throne from which He controls the universe are both mentioned several times."

Let me state the Qura'nic assertion, **Your Lord is God, who created the heavens and the earth in six days, then settled Himself on the Throne. 7:54p**

Several other verses also make the same assertion. The key words in these verses are days and throne. The Arabic word ayyam (days) has been interpreted not as a human day of twenty-four hours, but variously even by Western scholars, as ages, eons, epochs, or stages. All these definitions indicate a time of indeterminate duration.

The **Qurán** defines the day as:

The Angels and The Spirit ascend unto Him in a Day
The measure whereof is (as) fifty thousand years. 70:4

In another place, **Qurán** has this to say:

It is God who has created the heaven and the earth and all between them in six days. Then established Himself on the throne. He directs the affairs from the heavens to the earth, in the end all affairs will go up to Him, on a day that will last a thousand years of your reckoning. 32:4-5

Michael Sells in his remarkable book, APPROACHING THE QURA'N, while defining the day of reckoning has this to say about the Qura'nic day. "The word for day (yuam) also can be a more general term for any length of time or a moment in time, which is a time of indeterminate duration."

Thomas Cleary, in his admirable book, THE ESSENTIAL KORAN-THE HEART OF ISLAM, defines the Qura'nic day as an epoch. Other translations are ages, spans, eons, stages etc.

The other key word is throne. This again is like the day, an ayat, which has been variously defined as a symbol, a sign, a mystery, etc. The throne therefore can be defined in many ways, but definitely not as having a physical existence like a rich, kingly chair. The **Qurán** defines throne thus: **His throne does extend over the heavens and the earth. 2:225p**

A page earlier, the authors (Bloom and Blair) have this to say: "Among the sign passages, the great Throne verse" (2:225) is one of the most lyrical evocations of God's majesty:

God! There is no God but He-the Living, the Everlasting:

Neither slumber nor sleep seizes Him. To Him belongs all that is in heavens and on earth. Who is there that can intercede with Him except by His leave? He knows what is before them and what is after them.

And they comprehend nothing of His knowledge except as He wills His throne comprises the heavens and the earth, The preserving of them oppresses Him not He is the All-High The All Glorious? 2:255

Let me quote another sign passage about paradise:

Be quick in the race for forgiveness from your Lord And for a Garden whose width is that (of the whole) Of the heavens and of the earth, prepared for the righteous. 3:133

Thus, one cannot equate the Qura'nic concept of a day and the throne with the stories of the near Eastern cultures. Another point, if the Garden of Paradise is as wide as the heavens and the earth put together, where is the room for hell?

The eastern stream:

More important and relevant to my purpose is the other stream which is running through the Muslim world as a scourge, fed by a small brain-washed, bigoted, and intolerant minority. Its religious mentors have distorted the message of Islam to serve their own designs. They have caused the greatest damage to the Muslims of the world. They have put Islam under siege. They are the tools of obscurantism. They insist on the full strictness and rigor of religious beliefs and rites. This is theology not religion. Theology is manmade. Religion is inspired. The present day Wahabism- a puritanical and dogmatic sect of Islam-is the spiritual and ideological mentor of the Jihadists. They have overwhelmed the divine message and by-passed the **Qurán** by a clever stratagem. Their source of inspiration is the Shariah, a man-made body of laws developed in the first three or so centuries from the birth of Prophet Muhammad (PBUH) created about a thousand years ago and since frozen but still in practice. They have pulled down the Divine to their level instead of struggling to reach up to God which is their destiny.

Forever toiling towards your Lord, painfully toiling-but you shall meet Him. 84:6 There are as many Shariahs as there are sects and sub-sects, each claiming authenticity, each facing the other as a deadly opponent. The Shariah laws concentrate on issues of no importance. The **Qurán** anticipates such situations and warns:

But there are some people who vend frivolous tales,
To lead astray from the way of God, without any knowledge
And take the Book lightly. There is a degrading punishment
awaiting them. 31:6

Like the majority of clerics of other faiths these 'Mullahs'

Are selling God's signs for a petty price. 2:41 p

They are covering truth with falsehood, and concealing
The Truth knowingly. 2:42

And among them are illiterates who do not know the Book,
Only wishes, and who merely conjecture. 2:78

And are making a living by repudiating the Qurán. 56:82

Those who conceal any part of the Book that God has revealed, for
a little profit, take nothing but fire as food.
There are the ones who exchange error for guidance
And torment in place of forgiveness.
How great is their striving for fire?

That is because God has revealed the Book containing the truth,
but they seek causes of schism in the Book and
Have gone astray. 2:174p, 175, 176

The **Qurán** administers a strong warning to these misguided individuals.

Those who conceal The Clear (Signs) We have Sent down, and the
Guidance
After We have made it clear for the people in the Book-on them
shall be God's curse
and the curse of those entitled to curse. 2:159

The curse, I believe, is already in evidence in the misery and deprivation of the Muslim masses. This has been accomplished by their rulers by keeping their people illiterate, ignorant, oppressed, and poor. The so-called "Muslim fundamentalism" noticeable across the Muslim world is a reaction to the coercive political establishment, few opportunities for economic advancement and education, absence of rule of law and of good governance. Muslim societies are riven with dissensions and civil wars. Violence and extreme responses, such as suicide bombing, etc. are without foundation in their faith and are in total negation of the letter and spirit of Islam, a religion of peace and harmony, as you will certainly come to know after having read through this book.

One feature of the **Qurán** is that: **It was written down in the form of un-collated pieces** (INTRODUCTION TO THE QURA'N by M.A.S. Abdel Haleem.) The Book is organized neither in the order in which it was revealed nor theme- wise. Observations on the same subject are spread all over the Book and can be exploited to serve various purposes. To avert such misuse of the **Qurán** by any and all, I have selected in the first instance sixteen aspects and gathered in one place all that **Qurán** has to say on each of these subjects. This will help, I believe, in fuller and better understanding of the Divine message. These aspects are:

1. **Qurán** in its own eyes
2. The Divine defined.
3. Mission of Muhammad (P.B.U.H), the Prophet of Islam
4. **Qurán** and knowledge
5. Islam's relationship with other religions
6. Islam and Social justice

7. Islam and Jihad
8. Islam and Women
9. Islam and Terrorism
10. Justice
11. Environment
12. History
13. Economic Vision
14. Man's Genesis and Evolution
15. Creation of the Universes
16. Islam and Free Will Versus Determinism

From the list one would know how vital and relevant these subjects are in today's world.

There are myriad more areas which this book has not covered.

The Qura'nic verses have been reproduced without comments or background information such as occasion of revelation etc. This will enable the reader to concentrate on the message unfettered by external influences, hearsays, customs, traditions etc. The message is eternal and, I believe, should be read, interpreted and understood by the individual, according to his faith, state of knowledge, vision, wisdom, and perception.

There is no organization in Islam corresponding to the Roman Catholic Church in Christianity. There is no priestly hierarchy either; every Muslim must understand and act upon his beliefs according to his light. He is solely responsible to God on the day of reckoning for all his deeds. He has no savior and no intercessor.

The verses on some aspects are extensive. Certain exclusions have been made without affecting the total picture. Some verses lend themselves to being placed in more than one aspect. Hence, a repetition of certain verses is unavoidable.

The English rendition used by me is Abdulllah Yusuf Ali's THE MEANING OF THE HOLY QURA'N.

The references quoted in the book are explained as under:

The first numeral indicates the sura (chapter) of the **Qura'n** and the subsequent numbers indicate the verses. **2:162, 163** would mean chapter 2 and verses **162** and **163** of the **Qura'n**. The alphabet **p** attached at the end of a verse indicates part of a verse.

Chapter One

Qurán In Its Own Eyes

A message to all the worlds 68:52
Sent by Divine grace with Truth 42:17p

Guides mankind to ways of peace and safety,
Out of darkness into light
To a path that is straight. 5:16

A book of Signs 39:29 A Book to ponder 4:82

We have sent the Qurán in order
That you may learn wisdom and new knowledge. 12:2 and 40:2

A healing and a mercy 17:82p

The Qurán is a confirmation of revelations that went before it and
a fuller explanation. 10:37p
This Book is not for the illiterates. 2:7-8p

No one knows the Qurán's explanation but God
And those deeply rooted in knowledge. 3:7

Chapter 1

Qurán in Its Own Eyes

Qurán is an Arabic word meaning "reading." It is a collection and compilation of the Divine messages revealed to Prophet Muhammad (P.B.U.H) during the twenty-three (610-632 C.E.) years of his mission.

The **Qurán** is the sacred book of Islam just as the Torah (Old Testament) and the Injil (New Testament) are the sacred books of Judaism as revealed to the prophet Moses and Christianity as revealed to Jesus Christ. These scriptures are held in high esteem by the Muslims as well, and believing in them is a part of their faith.

The **Qurán** is the primary source of Islamic law and jurisprudence. Any matter contrary to the Qura'nic injunctions in letter and spirit is rejected by its followers.

The **Qurán** contains more than 77,000 words, divided into 114 chapters (Suras) and further subdivided into over 6,100 verses (Ayas.)

The **Qurán** calls itself by many names:

1. The **Qurán** This is the name most mentioned (in 46 verses)
2. **Book of Guidance, a Guide to Mankind 2:2, 3:4** and many other verses
3. **A Message to all the Worlds 38:87** and many other verses
4. **Mother of the Books 3:7** and other verses
5. **Book of Certain Truth 69:5** and many more
6. **Book of Power 13:31** and other verses
7. **Criterion 3:4** and other verses
8. **The Exposition 15:9** and other verses
9. **Pure and Holy 98:23** and other verses

10. **Most Honorable 56:77**
11. **A Message for the Heart 50:37**
12. **The Book that Makes Things Clear-The Perspicuous Book 12:1**
    and others
13. **Light 42:52**
14. **Inimitable 17:88**
15. **The Message 15:9** and other verses
16. **The Glorious Qurán 50:1** and other verses
17. **A Blessed Book 38:29**
18. **The Admonishing Qurán 38:1**
19. **Book that Confirms earlier Scriptures 54:8** and other verses
20. **Book of Wisdom 10:1** and other verses
21. **Book of Exalted Power 40:41**
22. **The Grand Qurán 15:87**
23. **A Wonderful Recital 72:1**
24. **The Word 86:13**
25. **Honored Pages 80:13**
26. **A Message of Instructions 80:11**
27. **Exalted 80:14**
28. **Immaculate 81:0**
29. **The Trust 33:72**
30. **A Reminder 80:11**
31. **Elevated 80:14**
32. **The Writ 27:1**
33. **A Book of Signs 39:29**
34. **A Book of Just Decrees 98:2-3**

God communicates with mankind by means of parables, oaths, ayas, similitudes, and allegories. Ayas and oaths have variously been defined as signs, symbols, mysteries, and reality behind appearances. The **Qurán** urges man to probe into these signs, to study the phenomena around him, to meditate upon them, to decipher them, to discover the laws governing them, and to know the causes of things etc. This effort, this striving will ultimately point to one Truth, to one Reality, the Eternal One, the unchanging Law. All of the **Qurán** therefore cannot be taken literally. Almost all of us settle for one dimensional reading. Literal **Qurán** is only the first level meant for the illiterates with primitive minds; they still form a substantial part of mankind.

They read the **Qurán** without insight which comes from knowledge. Advance in knowledge leads to refinement in the understanding and interpretation of the **Qurán**.

For full details please see Chapter 4.

Qurán is multidimensional and timeless. Many are its treasure houses. It is a varied book of many splendors, a book of guidance for all mankind, valid until the end of time. **Qurán** does not believe in form without content or belief without knowledge. In one sense, belief is concerned only with the appearances of things. Knowledge penetrates into the underlying reality.

<u>Not a New Religion</u>

The **Qurán** is emphatic in declaring that Islam, which means submission, is not a new religion. It is in the tradition of earlier messages sent to mankind through many prophets-**Qurán** names twenty-five of them-Noah to Abraham to Moses to Jesus and finally to Muhammad. (P.B.U.H) **Qurán** also confirms earlier scriptures.

Nothing is said to you which has not been said

To other apostles before you. 41:43p

We sent the Torah which contains guidance and light. 5:44p

Later in the train of prophets, we sent Jesus, son of Mary, confirming the Torah which has been sent down before him and gave him the gospel containing guidance and light. 5:46p

Note: There are many more pronouncements on this subject, the important ones have been brought together in Chapter 5.

The **Qurán** although verifies and confirms the core messages earlier prophets brought to their peoples and yet it differs with other scriptures in some vital aspects. Some of these are briefly mentioned.

The Qura'nic concept of God is varied and complex, evolving with human knowledge and universal unlike the concept of God in Judaism, Christianity, Hinduism and Zoroastrianism etc. This point finds elaboration in Chapter 2.

The **Qurán** has been preserved in its original purity and authenticity. This is not the case with other scriptures. These have been altered, added or deleted in substantial measure.

We did take a covenant with the Christians;

But they forgot a good part of the message that was sent to them. 5:14p

Biblical scholars have called the New Testament in its present form the "Gospel of St. Paul" and the "Gospel of the Roman Church." Some have called it "a cult of three equal gods" –far from the monotheism of Jesus Christ who believed in Jewish monotheism. The Old Testament?

The children of Israel changed the word from their right places and forgot a good part of the message sent to them. 5:13 p

Today's Torah (Old Testament) has more to do with brilliant rabbis like Ezras (10th century), and Saadia Ben Joseph, and Jayyumi (892-942), and Moses Ben Maimon (1135-1204) than Prophet Moses. These rabbis were born, grew up, and worked in Muslim lands, and I suspect have been influenced by the **Qurán** and the Islamic civilization which was then at its peak.

In short, the two scriptures have lost their divine character somewhere down the lane.

A Universal Message

The **Qurán** is a universal message addressed to all mankind. It is not specific to any tribe, nation, region, community, or a group of people. This aspect finds mention in many verses. Some are quoted below.

We have sent down the Book to you with the truth for all mankind. 39:41p

A book which We have revealed to you that you may lead mankind out of darkness into light. 14:1p

But it is nothing less than a message to all the worlds. 10:37p, 27:192

Blessed is the One Who revealed the Criterion
To a servant of the Divine for it to be a warning
To all peoples. 25:1, 81:27

We have explained in detail in this Qurán
For the benefit of mankind every kind of similitude.
But man is contentious in most things. 18:54

Other Important Features

Book of Signs

The **Qurán** is a book of signs. The divine communicates with humans through signs-clues to the mystery of reality, oaths, parables, similitudes, symbols, homilies, and allegories. **A Book whose signs are confirmed then explained from One Who is most wise and aware. 11:1**

We shall show them (the unbelievers) our signs in the horizons
And within themselves,
Until it is clear to them that it is the truth. 41:53p
Only those who understand parables have knowledge. 29:43

The messenger of Islam: **was sent to mankind to rehearse His signs to man and instruct him in scripture, wisdom, and new knowledge. 2:151** These signs (the **Qurán** recounts more than one-hundred signs):**are self-evident in the heart of those endowed with knowledge. 29:49**

God shows His signs; how many of God's signs will you then deny? 40:81
Indeed, we have propounded for men, in this Qurán, every kind of parable.
But if you bring a sign to the unbelievers they are sure to say it. "You do nothing but talk vanities." 30:58

Let me quote Michael Sells (APPROACHING THE QURA'N) on the subject: "The complex Qura'nic sound patterns and the relation of sound to meaning, what we might call 'the sound vision' of the **Qurán** are brought out and cultivated in Qura'nic recitation. No translations can fully capture this sound vision. The translations have attempted to bring across the lyricism of the hymnic passages.

This lyricism is related to the use of oaths involving a key set of what the **Qurán** considers "Signs," (ayas) clues to the mystery of reality. These signs include the patterns of day and night, male and female, odd and even, singular and plural. The Arabic construction of these oaths can be translated in a number of ways. I have used the phrase "by the" as in Sura 89 1-5:

By the dawn, by the nights ten, by the odd and even
By the night as it eases away
Is there not in that an oath for the thoughtful mind?"

Because of these oaths and signs, the **Qurán** lends itself to multiple levels of meaning. To fully understand its message, the **Qurán** demands from its readers: knowledge, faith, wisdom, understanding, and full application of reason and logic. The **Qurán** seeks at times to communicate its message by referring to history, archaeology, the natural world around us, and the cosmic phenomenon.

It is for this reason that the **Qurán's** audience is the educated.

This Book is not for the illiterates, they know not the Book and seek their own desires and indulge in conjectures. 2:78

When Qurán is recited to those who are given knowledge they fall down on their faces in humble prostration. 17:107p

And it is so that those to whom knowledge has been given may know that it is the truth from your Lord. 22:54p

God has revealed the Book to you. In it are verses basic or fundamental.
They are the foundations of the Book
Others are not of well-established meaning
No one knows its true meanings except God,
And those who are firmly grounded in knowledge
None will grasp the message except men of understanding. 3:7p

Hence, the limits of human experience and state of knowledge at a particular time in human evolution defines the way we understand and interpret the **Qurán.** With the increase in human knowledge, the understanding of the **Qurán** also gains in depth. (For full details, see Chapter 4 and later part of this chapter.)

The **Qurán** defines God's signs:
Indeed! In the creation of heavens and the earth;
And the alternation of the Night and Day;
And the ships that sail the sea for the benefit of humanity,
And the water God sends down from the sky,
With which God enlivens the earth after its death and distributes all kind of animals thereupon and the coursing of the winds, and the clouds employed between sky and earth
Surely there are signs for people who are wise. 2:164

It is God who has made the sun shine and the moon glow,
And determined lunar phases that you may know
The number of the years and the calculation.
God did not create that in any way but right;
God makes these signs clear to people who know. 10:5

God is the one who sends you down
Water from the sky, from which there is drink,
And vegetation for grazing, God produces grain for you thereby,
And olives, and date palms, and grapes, and all kinds of fruit
Surely in that is a sign for people who reflect. 16:10-11

Don't they look at the birds, suspended in the air, in the sky?
Nothing holds them up but God.
Surely there are signs in that for people who believe. 16:79

Haven't they traveled the earth
And seen how those before them ended up?
They were more powerful than these and they tilled the soil in great numbers than these have done.
And when their messengers came to them
With clear signs they rejected them to their own destruction.
It was not God who wronged them; rather, they wronged themselves,

Then the end of those who did evil will be the worse, as they repudiated the signs of God, and used to deride them. 30:9-10

The parable of those who take protectors other than God

Is that of the spider who builds a house but truly flimsiest of houses. 29:41p

But such are the Parables We set for mankind,
But only those understand them who have knowledge. 29:43

Even the Word "day" is a Sign Word

The angels and the Spirit ascend to Him in a day;
The measure whereof is as fifty thousand years. 70:4

God's Throne is a parable, so is Paradise

His throne does extend over heavens and the earth. 2:255p
Be quick in the race for forgiveness from your Lord,
And for a paradise extending over the heavens and the earth
Prepared for the righteous. 3:133

The Stories of Prophets

The stories of prophets and their miracle are allegorical and not to be treated literally. They are parables narrated to convey a lesson, a moral.

In Joseph and his brothers are signs for seekers. 12:7
There came to you Moses with clear signs.
Yet you (his people) worshiped the calf. 2:92p
Moses put your hand into your armpit, it will come out white without disease as another sign. 20:22
That We may show you some of our major signs, go to pharaoh for he is tyrannical. 20:23-24
Surely in the story of Abraham there is a sign but most of them are not believers. 26:102

So we delivered Noah and those with him in the loaded ark and drowned the rest of them. There is a sign in this, yet many of them are not believers. 26:119-121

Similarly the stories of Saleh (26:158) and Lot (26:174) and Shuaib (26:109) are parables.

**We will show them Our signs in the horizon
And within themselves. 41:53p**

It is clear that a person's understanding of the book depends on his ability to unravel these signs, parables, stories, similitudes etc. Every natural phenomenon surrounding man and the celestial bodies are signs. Evolution in nature, including man, the ruins and the remnants of past civilizations, paradise, hell, God's throne, Day of Judgment, creation of the universe, human soul, human spirit, and many more elements that have an impact on human life are signs (ayas) awaiting probing to discover the reality behind appearances.

And the fate of those who reject or subvert or repudiate the signs etc. of God?

As for those who try to subvert our signs there is a punishment most humiliating. 34:5

**No one rejects our signs except the unjust. 29:49
Then the end of those who did evil will be the worse, as they repudiated the signs of God, and used to deride them. 30:9-10**

**Therefore, evil was the end of those who did evil,
For they denied the signs of God and made fun of them. 30:10**

**We helped (Noah) against people who rejected Our signs,
They were a people given to evil; so we drowned them all. 21:77**

**And for those who repudiate the signs of God
There is a severe torment for them. 3:4p**

They have rejected our signs and vain are their deeds. 7:147

A bad example are those who rejected Our signs,

And who oppressed their own souls. 7:177

The message is a reminder as man is forgetful.

Assuredly this is a reminder for anyone who wants to remember. 80:11

A Book of Guidance, Mercy, and Blessings, Glad News, and Warnings

This is the Book let there be no doubt about it, in it is guidance for: The conscientious, who believe in the unseen, who are constant in prayers. Spend on others out of what God has provided them And who believe in the revelation sent down to you (Muhammad) And what was revealed before you, who are certain of the Hereafter They follow guidance from their Lord, and they are the successful ones. 2:2-5

These are the signs of the Qurán, a clarifying Book in itself And clearly showing the truth. A guide and glad news for the believers. Those who are consistent in prayers and spend to eliminate poverty And are certain of the life to come. 27:1-3

For those who believe Qurán is a guidance and a healing. 41:44p

When the Qurán is read, listen to it with attention and silently So that you may receive mercy. 7:204

The Qurán is a healing and a mercy to those who believe. To the unjust it causes nothing but loss after loss. 17:82

Say, "It has been sent by divine grace from your Lord with truth, As a guide and glad tiding'." 16:02 p

There are insights for humanity and guidance And mercy for people who are sure. 45:20

Verily this Qurán guides to that which is most sound And gives glad news to the believers who do good deeds

They shall have a great reward. 17:9

We have sent you a Book full of blessings. 38:29p

And it certainly is a guide and a mercy

To those who believe. 27:77

The word "believer" occurs many times in these verses. It is time to define the qualities that go to constitute a believer. A believer is one who:

    i.   **Is conscious of God**
    ii. **Believes in the unseen**
    iii. **Is constant in prayers**
    iv. **Spends on others out of what God has provided him**
    v. **Believes in what was revealed to you and what was revealed before your time**
    vi. **And has the assurance of the hereafter 2:2p, 3-4**

The Muslims, the Jews, the Christians, and the Sabians,
And any who believe in God and the last day and do good
Have their reward with their Lord. There is nothing for them to fear;
They will not sorrow 2:62 and 5:69
As for the Muslims, the Jews, the Sabians, the Christians, the Magians, (Zoroastrians)* and the polytheists, God will decide among them on the day of resurrection. 22:17p

Any who denies God, His angels, His Books,
His Messengers and the Day Of Judgment has gone far, far astray. 4:136

It is abundantly clear that Muslims, Jews, Christians, and Zoroastrians are believers. Polytheists? It is not for us humans to judge them. The divine has reserved this authority to Himself.

Righteousness as an element in the life of a believer occurs many times. Who is righteous? The Qura'nic answer is:

---

* Zoroastrians are the followers of the prophet Zoroaster of Persia who is said to have preached around 500 BCE.

It is not righteousness that you turn your faces towards East or West.
But it is righteousness-To believe in God, and the Last Day
And the Angels, the scriptures and the prophets,
And spend of your wealth out of love for God, among your kin,
The orphans, the needy traveler, and the poor.
And for freeing the slaves; and are steadfast in prayers,
And establish regular charity, and fulfill the contracts they have made.
And those who are patient in misfortune and affliction and hard times.
Such are the people of truth and God fearing. 2:177

Is there anything in these verses to exclude the followers of other faiths from being righteous?

The **Qurán** was revealed in stages. **We have revealed the Qurán to you by stages. 76:23**

Those who reject faith say, "Why was not the Qurán revealed to him all at once?" It is this way so We may strengthen your heart thereby, and We have rehearsed it to you in slow, distinct, and orderly stages. 25:32

We have divided the Qurán into parts that you may recite it to men slowly with deliberation.

We have revealed it by stages. 17:106

Qurán is Pure

The **Qurán** was revealed in the full light of history and preserved within the year of the passing away of the Prophet. It was, however, organized in a book form and copies made out in the reign of Usman, the third caliph, a son-in-law and a close and lifelong companion of Muhammad. (P.B.U.H) Thus the purity and authenticity of the message has been preserved for all time to come, which is a unique feature of the **Qurán**. The **Qurán** itself guarantees its purity:

A book well- guarded   56:78
We have sent down this exposition and We are actually guarding
it. 15:9
This is indeed the Glorious Qurán inscribed in a tablet preserved.
85:21-22

If he (the Prophet) falsely attributed some sayings to Us, We would
seize him by the right hand and sever his aorta. And none could
prevent it.   69:44-47

A messenger from God reciting immaculate scrolls
In which are just decrees. 98:23

Falsehood cannot reach it from any side. 41:42 p

The **Qurán** is best recited to understand the resonance of the sound
pattern and the power and beauty of the language. When the book is
recited, a calm descends on the listeners, and they feel relaxed.

**When the Qurán is read, listen to it with attention. And hold your
peace so that you may receive mercy.   7:204**

The **Qurán** is the primary source of Islamic law and jurisprudence,
beliefs and practices. Any matter contrary to the Qura'nic injunctions
and pronouncements is rejected by its followers.

The **Qurán** is of divine origin, as the book claims, and its language
cannot be equaled in its intensity, sublimity, dignity, and magnificence.

**And this Qurán is not something that could be produced
By other than God. 10:37p**

**Do they say, "He (Muhammad) composed it?"
Say, "Then bring a chapter like it
And call upon anyone other than God,
if you are truthful." 10:38**

Note: George Sale, a devout Christian priest who was the first to
translate the **Qurán** into English directly from Arabic in 1734 C.E.,
describes the style of the **Qurán** as "generally beautiful and fluent in

many places. . . sublime and magnificent. It must not be supposed that the translation comes up to the dignity of the original."

This problem is being faced even today. The consensus is that the **Qurán** can only be approached and does not lend itself fully to rendition in another language.

No Compulsion, Entry into Islam is Voluntary and Conscious

We have sent a Book for mankind according to truth. So whoever accepts guidance does so to the benefit of his own soul and whoever strays strays only to the detriment of his own soul and you are not the one to dispose of their affairs. 39:41

So if they turn away we have not sent you as a guard over them. Your only duty is to convey the message. 42:48p and 2 others

Say, "I do not have the powers to do you harm or guide you right." 73:21

The prophet declares:

You have your way and I have my way. 109:6

Is it not to God that sincere obedience is due? Yet those who take protectors other than God say we only worship them that they may draw us nearer to God. God will judge between them as to their differences. 39:3p

Say, "Everyone acts according to his disposition.
But your Lord alone knows who is best guided on the way." 17:84

Thus it is not given to man to judge between the followers of different ways. This is the privilege of God.

We only sent you to give glad tidings and warnings. 25:56

Let there be no compulsion in religion.
Truth stands out clear from error.
Whoever rejects evil and believes in God
Has grasped the most trustworthy hand hold

That never breaks. 2:256p

And to rehearse the Qurán and if any accept guidance they do it for the good of their own soul and if any stray say, "I am only a warner." 27:92

The Truth

We sent down the Qurán in truth and in truth has it descended. 17:105p

The revelation of the Book, in which there is no doubt,
Is from the Lord of the universe. Do they perchance say "He made it up?"
No, this is the truth from your Lord. 32:2-3p

But those to whom knowledge has been given
See that what has been sent down to you from your Lord is the truth. 34:6p

That which We have revealed to you by inspiration of the Book
Is the truth-confirming what was revealed before it. 35:31p

For We have revealed the Book to you In truth; so serve God sincerely in your way of life. 39:2p

Verily this (the Qurán) is the very truth of assured certainty. 56:95, 69:51

We have sent you the Book for Mankind,
according to truth. 39:41p

God has sent the Book in truth. 42:17p

What has been revealed to Mohammad is the truth from their Lord. 47:2p

This is no less than a message to the universe.
And you shall certainly know the truth of it,
after a while. 38:87-88

Book of Exalted Power and Wisdom

And indeed it is a book of exalted powers. 41:41p

In honored pages exalted and immaculate. 80:11

These are the verses of the Book of wisdom.
10:1, 12:2, and 31:2

By the Qurán full of wisdom. 36:2 and 43:4p

For God has sent down to you the Book and wisdom and taught you
what you did not know. And to you the grace of God is great. 4:113p

Inimitable

Say, "Even if humans and spirits all gathered together to produce
Something like this Qurán. They could not produce anything like it
Even if they help each other." 17:88
Do they say, "He forged it?" Say, "Then bring a chapter like this
And call to your aid anyone other than God if what you say is true."
10:38

Most Honorable, Without Crookedness

I swear by setting of the stars-and this is a tremendous oath, if you
only knew-
This is indeed a Qurán most honorable, inscribed in a well-guarded
Book
Which none can touch but those who are clean. 56:75-80

This is indeed the word of a noble messenger. 69:40

The book without crookedness. 18:1p

A Qurán without any crookedness. 39:28

Praise be to God who revealed a book to a devotee without
crookedness so it is straight. 18:1-2

It is a Qurán in Arabic without any crookedness in order that they may guard against evil. 39:28

<u>Makes Things Clear, Easy, Consistent, and Without Discrepancy</u>

By the Book that makes things clear. 44:2

This is a message and a Qurán making things clear. 36:69p

By the Book that makes things clear we have made it a Qurán in Arabic
That you may understand. 43:23
These are the signs of the Book, a Qurán that clarifies things. 15:1 also 27:1
So We have just made it (The Qurán) easy
By using your language that they may heed. 44:58
And we have made the Qurán
Easy to understand and remember. 54:17p, 22p, 32p, 40p

Do they not ponder on the Qurán-were it from other than God,
They would have found much discrepancy in it. 4:82

God has revealed (from time to time)the most beautiful message
In the form of a Book Consistent with itself,
And repeating in various aspects. 39:23p

<u>Glorious, Discriminating, a Message for the Heart</u>
This is indeed a discriminating word and not to be spoken in jest. 86:13-14

But this is a glorious Qurán. 85:21 and 50:1

Indeed this is a message for any that has,
A heart and understanding or lends an ear and is a witness. 50:37

No, there are signs that are clear in the hearts of those
Endowed with knowledge. 29:49p

Law

The law governing the universe has been:

Inscribed in a record clear to those who can read.
These laws are eternal. 33:62p, 17:77p, 35:43-8

Man is thus charged with the responsibility of discovering the law and the law governing his own existence so that he lives according to it, lives without conflict with nature, with himself and his fellow beings. This is the straight way, the way of God, the way of the universal law. **Only those understand parables who have knowledge. 29:43**

In this Book are verses basic and clear in meaning, others are not entirely clear...their true meaning is known to God and those among men who are firmly grounded in knowledge: men of understanding. 3:7p

Thus they alone understand the Message who are highly educated, the wise, people with high intellect, the philosophers, men of letters, the historians, the economists, the scientists, the inspired ones, the Nobel laureates. These privileged human beings alone are competent to interpret the **Qurán**.

There is therefore no finality in the meaning of the message which is complex with layers and layers to comprehend. With human knowledge increasing every day, the meaning and significance of the **Qurán** gains depth. As of now, and for many epochs to come when human knowledge may have vastly expanded, the understanding of the **Qurán** must remain tentative.

This subject finds comprehensive mention in Chapter 4.

Protocol of Recitation of the **Qurán**

O you folded in garments (refers to Muhammad P.B.U.H)
Stand through the night but not all night
Half of it or a little less or a little more
And recite the Qurán in slow, measured,
And rhythmic tones. 73:1-4

**When the Qurán is read, listen to it with attention
And hold your peace: that you may receive mercy. 7:204**

Only the clean to touch the Book. 56:79

This Exalted Book of Wisdom also has its Limitations

Even if there were a Qurán by which mountains were moved

**And the earth were cloven or the dead were made to speak.
Nonetheless the command is entirely with God. 13:31p**

Mode of Communication

Muslim theologians are more or less unanimous in stating that Gabriel is God's chosen instrument for communicating the Message to Muhammad, (P.B.U.H) His messenger and votary. They also maintain that Gabriel is an angel, but these opinions find no support in the **Qurán**.

**It is not given to man that God should speak to him
Otherwise than through sudden inspiration or from behind a veil
Or by sending a prophet to reveal by divine permission, God's will.
God is exalted and wise. 42:51**

Indeed, "revelations," "sent down", or "inspiration," all three words carry the same meaning and are the words used to indicate the mode of communication of the message.

**And that is how we inspired you spiritually by our order
Before this you did not know what revelation was,
what faith was. And we have caused this message
to be a light wherewith We guide whom we will of our servants so
that they guide man to the straight way-the way that leads to the
Divine. 42:52**

**If We wished, We would take away what We have revealed to you
by inspiration. 17:86p**

With God is the beginning and the end of all things. 42:53p

By His command does He send the spirit of inspiration
To any of His servants He pleases
That it may warn men of the day of mutual meeting. 40:15p
Verily this is a revelation from the Lord of the worlds
With it come down the spirit of faith and truth to your heart and
mind:
So that you may admonish in the perspicuous
Arabic tongue. 26:192-5
The revelation of the Book Is from God
The exalted in power, full of wisdom. 46:2
Verily it is We who have revealed the
Book to you in truth. 39:2p, 4:105

Thus does God send down the inspiration to you
And those before you, God the Mighty, the Wise. 42:2
Thus We have sent by inspiration to you an
Arabic Qurán. 42:7p

By the star when it goes down
Your companion is neither astray nor being mislead
Nor does he speak of his own desire. It is no less than
Inspiration sent down to him.
He was taught by One mighty in Power imbued with wisdom
While he was in the highest part of the horizon
Then He approached and came closer and was at a distance of
Two bow lengths or nearer. So did God convey
The inspiration to His servant what
He meant to convey. 53:1-10

It is a wonder for people that We inspired a man
From among them to warn humanity. 10:2p

Say, "What has come to me by inspiration
Is that your God is one God.
Will you therefore bow to His will?" 21:108

Say, "I am but a man like you. But inspiration has come to me
That your deity is one God-

So whoever hopes to meet his Lord should act with integrity
And not compromise with anyone the worship of his Lord." 18:110

We have revealed to our servant. 2:23p
This is a revelation from the Lord of the worlds
With it came down, the spirit of faith and trust (Ruhul-amin)
26:192-3

The words "revealed," "sent down," and "inspiration," carry the same meaning and are used about a hundred times to describe the way the message was communicated. Against this, Gabriel is mentioned only once:

Say, "Whoever is hostile to Gabriel who revealed this to you by God's leave,
Confirming what preceeded as guidance and good news to the believers." 2:97

Who was Gabriel? Was he an angel?

O prophet, tell your two wives if they turn to God in repentance it is better.

Your hearts have been impaired and if you assist one another against him,

Then surely his helper is God and Gabriel and the righteous believers

And besides them the angels are his supporters. 66:4p

In verse **2:98**, Gabriel is mentioned again:

Whoever is hostile to God and God's angels and messengers

And Gabriel and Michael, God is hostile to the ungrateful. 2:98

Thus, in both the verses, Gabriel (twice) and Michael (once) are mentioned separately from angels which points to their being entities apart and distinct from angels and denies the Muslim clerics' contention that Gabriel is an angel.

Thus only once Gabriel (**2:97**) is mentioned as the one: **Who revealed this to you.** The words "inspiration," "revealed," and "sent down," are used many times. In any case, Gabriel is not an angel. Angels are invisible beings, beyond human perception. Angels are inferior to man. They bowed to Adam (for details see chapter 4.) How can an angel be a teacher to a human being, the best and the finest of mankind?

Let us look at this verse.

It is no less than inspiration sent down to him.
He was taught by one mighty in power, endowed with Wisdom
For He appeared while He was in the highest part of the horizon.
Then He approached and came closer
And was at a distance of but two bow lengths or nearer.
So did God convey the inspiration to his servant
Conveyed what he meant to convey. 53:1-8

Endowed with wisdom and mighty in power are attributes reserved exclusively for God. (In **42:2** and more than one hundred verses) How could Gabriel be wise and mighty? All this points to the fact that the revelation was conveyed directly from God to the prophet of Islam.

Our Islamic clerics are guilty once again of violating the **Qurán**. The **Qurán** mentions Ruhul-Amin (the spirit of trust) once in 26:193 (already quoted) and Ruhul-Quds (the Holy Spirit) twice, in 2:87p and 2:253.

We gave Jesus, the son of Mary, clear signs and
And strengthened him with the Holy Spirit. 2:87p, 2:253P

In both the cases, the Holy Spirit, (Ruhul-Quds) relates to Jesus Christ. Our Islamic theologians equate the two "ruhs" with Gabriel. This again is not supported by the **Qurán**.

And what is Spirit (ruh?)

They ask you about spirit (ruh)Say, 'Spirit is from the command of my Lord.
Man cannot understand its nature;'
Since you have been given but a little knowledge. 17:85

If "ruh" or spirit is beyond man's comprehension, it is preposterous to suggest that ruh refers to Gabriel.

Night journey (Isra) by the prophet is another vital event in the spiritual and mystical development of the prophet, perhaps similar to the one experienced by Moses on Mount Sinai. Let us see what the **Qurán** says about the night journey.

Glory to the One Who transported His servant by night from the Sacred mosque
To the farthest mosque the environment of which We had blessed
So that We might show him some of Our signs;
For He alone is all-hearing and all-seeing. 17:1

The Sacred Mosque stands identified as being in Mecca (see 2:144, 1:49. 1:50, and 9:18 etc.) but what about the farthest mosque? The Muslim clerics have identified the farthest mosque as a place of worship in Jerusalem which is a thousand or so miles away from Mecca. At the time of the revelation of these verses, Jerusalem had two places of worship a wall, a remnant of the Temple of Solomon sacred to the Jews, and the Church of the Sepulcher, a place of worship sacred to the Christians. Where is the place that God has blessed and raised its status to match with the status of the prophet? How far is the farthest in divine scale? A million light years?

Let us seek an explanation from the **Qurán**.

By the star when it descends your companion has not erred
And has not gone astray. Nor does he speak of his own free will
It is an inspiration with which he is inspired
One mighty in Power taught him.
Endowed with wisdom he acquired poise and balance
And reached the highest part of the horizon.
Then he approached and came near, as close as two bow lengths or closer
When He revealed to His servant what He revealed
His heart did not falsify what he perceived.
Will you then dispute with him what he saw?
For indeed he saw Him on another descent near the lote tree
When mystery shrouded the lote tree

Beyond which none may pass, close to the garden of eternity. His gaze did not deviate or stray
He truly saw some of the greatest signs of His lord. 53:1-18

These verses define the farthest point-near the lote tree. Beyond, all is veiled in mystery. This lote tree is near the garden of tranquility, beyond which none can pass. It does mark the limit of man's reach and beyond is the domain of the Absolute. And this was the place God had blessed. And what was the purpose of this night journey?
  a. To reveal to His servant what He meant to convey and
  b. To show some of His greatest signs
  c. To reveal the divine secrets to His chosen messenger **72:26P-27P**

Now read the verses on night journey.

Glory to the one who transported His servant by night from the Sacred mosque
To the farthest mosque the environment of which We had blessed
So that We might show him some of our signs;
For He alone is all-hearing and all-seeing. 17:1

Verses 53:1-18 are a commentary on the night journey. After this event the prophet was fully equipped to carry out his mission and comprehended some of the greatest signs of God, and was given some more of wisdom and new knowledge, insight into the mysteries of the universe.

We have sent to you a messenger from among you,
Who rehearses Our signs to you
And purifies you and instructs you in scripture and wisdom
And in new knowledge. 2:151
Without doubt, he saw Him on the clear horizon. And he is not grudging with the knowledge of the unseen. 81:23,24

Please be assured that it was Muhammad that had approached the divine. This verse identifies not only the farthest part of the horizon, but it talks of the signs of God which were shown to the ultimate human. For the prophet this could well be the greatest spiritual experience of his life. Tales the Muslim clerics wound around this event are fantasies and an attempt to mislead the Muslims and others.

Qurán anticipates such misguided individuals and warns:

Those who conceal the clear signs We have sent down, and the guidance
After we have made it clear for the people in the Book-
On them shall be God's curse and the curse of those entitled to curse. 2:159
And among them are illiterates who do not know the Book
Only wishes and who merely conjecture. 2:78
And are making a living by repudiating the Qurán. 56:82
They are covering truth with falsehood
And concealing the truth knowingly. 2:42

During the earlier centuries of Islam, vending of such amusing tales may have been justified. Islam was rapidly embracing people from all creeds, faiths, and religions living in North Africa and the Middle East. Even the followers of witch doctors! There was perhaps a need for incorporating such folklore to popularize Islam as well as to retain the new converts in the Islamic faith and to accommodate some of their sensitivities, popular customs etc. But in today's world, such accretions are blasphemous, defame Islam, and they should be taken out of our books.

Understanding the **Qurán**

I have found the following principles helpful in comprehending the **Qurán**.

1. The **Qurán** has been compiled neither time-wise nor theme-wise. Observations and guidance on a subject are found scattered at different places in the **Qurán**. It will be highly useful if observations on the same subject are gathered together in one place and the picture is seen in its totality. This will enable you to know which colors dominate, which are significant, and which have minor representation. Please do not fragment the **Qurán** to suit your convenience. That is the principle I have observed in this book.

2. Muslim scholars are of the opinion that a Qura'nic verse is best understood if the time and circumstances and the event that triggered

a verse are known. In spite of the massive research undertaken in the first few centuries of the birth of Islam, their success is minimal. Less than one per cent of the verses have been placed in these frames that too of doubtful authenticity and smack of conjecture. **Qurán** is an eternal book providing guidance for mankind up to the end of time. Why shackle it with extraneous influences? Why put constraints on it? Each generation of mankind must be free to understand it and interpret it according to his conscience and knowledge. There is no priesthood in Islam, everybody is responsible for himself to God.

3. **Qurán** is not a book of history. Historic references are only illustrative, meant to convey a lesson, a moral imperative, or to elucidate a point. Similarly, the story of prophets and the miracles vouchsafed to them are signs. (Please see Chapter 3 for a full discussion.)

4. The **Qurán** is the best commentary upon itself:

A Book with verses fundamental, explained in detail by One Who is wise. 1:1p God has revealed the most beautiful message in the form of a Book conformable in its juxtaposition and yet repeating 39:23p A Book whose verses are explained in detail. 41:2

5. **Qurán** is a miracle of miracles. Its meaning, interpretation, significance and depth of understanding evolves and develops with human experience and knowledge. Human evolution and state of civilization therefore defines the way we understand it. At any time, therefore, the interpretation of the **Qurán** is tentative. The finality may come, if at all, when man has mastered all knowledge and unraveled all the signs of God. It is only then that man would fully grasp the truth, the reality, the light, and the law that God is and the Book of Wisdom.

6. Most importantly, the **Qurán** expects you to ponder over it (4:82)

It is: **A Book whose verses are confirmed,
Then explained in detail from One Who is
Most wise and aware. 11:1**
Qurán thus offers its own explanation and no outside assistance is required to understand the Book.

Chapter Two

THE DIVINE DEFINED

All upon earth perishes, but the face of God endures forever, majestic, sublime and giving. 55:26
Each day the Divine shines in new splendor. 55:29p
Even if all the trees on earth were pens and the ocean augmented by seven more oceans were ink, the words of God would not be exhausted in the writing.   31:27
Everyone has an aim
To which God gives direction.
So strive in everything good. Wherever you all are, God will bring you together. 2:148p

He is God, one God forever not begetting, un-begotten, and having as an equal none. 112
God is truly kind and merciful to humanity. 22:65p
The Divine Law is immutable. 35:43p
God is the Reality, the Light, the Truth. 30:31p, 24:35p, 21:44p

They have not truly assessed the measure of God.
God is transcendent beyond
Any association they make. 39:67p
O Soul in repose, return to your Lord,
Pleased and accepted, join the company of my servants,
Enter into My Garden. 89:27-30

Chapter 2

The Divine Defined

Gods, goddesses, idols, deities etc. enjoying divine status have been central to all religions, faiths, creeds, believes etc. since a particular life form evolved into a human-Adam. It is so even today. God is also the central phenomenon around which the religion of Islam rotates, but the Islamic God is unique in some ways. He is uncompromisingly monotheistic. He is universal: God of the universe, God of all mankind, not the deity of any race or nation, or creed or belief. He is infinite and timeless. He is dynamic, developing, and evolving, from the elemental concept of a Being into highly complex and mystical concepts. **Each day He shines in new splendor. 55:29p**

At the base He is a personal God who controls human destiny. He is the Light, the Law, the ultimate Reality, and the Truth at the apex. And in between there are many levels. He is the source of wisdom, knowledge, and justice. He is creator par excellence.

The primitive human being living in the inaccessible jungles of the world will find comfort and solace in the Islamic God. The vast majority of the human beings living in the civilized and not so civilized societies also believe in a personal God, a Being with whom they can relate, seek solace and refuge, offer sacrifices to propitiate Him, build places simple and majestic to honor Him, where they can congregate to pray and worship their version of a deity. Islamic God responds to their urgings as well. He is the God of the mystics, the Sufis, the metaphysicians, the philosophers, the educated, and the highly educated. In short, every man seeks in Him what he needs to meet his temporal and mental needs, to satisfy his spiritual and inner urgings. Even atheists like Richard Dawkins (author of THE GOD DELUSION) will find in the Qura'nic

God many aspects which will cast serious doubt on his conviction that God does not exist. Has he defined God which he believes does not exist or was never born in the first instance? It is too simplistic to deny the existence of something because science in its present stage of development is unable to prove it. This is to deny the infinite possibilities of human imagination-"the ability to think of what is not" (Jean Paul Sartre.) Has man's imagination reached its limit? Has he exhausted the limitless potentials of his mind and body and spirit and inspiration? Is there no more progress in human knowledge? Has mankind ceased to invent? Is Dawkins sure that tomorrow's knowledge will not demolish his pet theories? Has his well of inspiration dried? Is Mr. Dawkins under the delusion that he has understood the mystery and pathos of life? The world will continue to produce Platos, Socrates, Aristotles, Voltairs, Bacons, Karl Marxs, Shakespeares, Kants, Bertrand Russels, Newtons, Einsteins, Ibn-Khalduns, Avicennas, Omar Khayyams, Rumis, Hasan al-Marraqushias, Nasier ud-Din al-Tiusis, Avu'l Fath al-Khuzinis, Abu Abdakkah Muhammad al-Idrisis, Abu'l Abbas of Seville, Abu Marwan ibn Zuhrs of Seville, known to Europeans and the medical world as Avenzoar, Al-Ghazalis, Averroes, Toynbees to name only a few geniuses. Every age has produced Dawkins' and quickly forgotten them. They are an ephemeral phenomenon. Their contribution to human civilization is zero, if not negative. The true measure of God is yet to be determined. What is Dawkins denying then? He and the ilk of him are aware only of the God of Christianity which is one third of a trinity, or the God of Judaism who is God only of prophet Israel, his twelve sons, and their descendants. Their knowledge of the God of Islam is limited to the basic level. They are unaware of His evolving nature and His complexity.

Qura'nic God creates, and establishes order, proportion, and balance within His creation. He ordains laws that govern the universe. His laws are eternal and immutable. He creates and grants guidance to mankind. **Qurán** is a book of guidance.

God is the Evolver, the Fashioner. He is dynamic, evolving perpetually. Every day He shines in new splendor. God is the Light, the Reality, the Law, the Truth. If man fails to discover the law of God and follow it in his living, as everything else in His creation is doing, he could be blotted out and replaced by beings new and unrecognizable to today's man.

God forever, not begetting, unbegotten, having as an equal, none. Eternal, self-subsisting, supporter of all, knower of the hidden and the open. Limitless in His glory, sublime, indefinable, omnipotent, omniscient, omnipresent, sustainer of the worlds, most compassionate, most caring, and most forgiving, forgiving of all sins of man. Beginning and end of all. Free of all wants and independent of all the creatures of the world. Beyond the reach of a created being's perception, most generous, irresistible, and eternal.

All upon earth perishes, but the face of God endures forever, majestic, sublime, and giving. 55:26

Uncaused cause of all being. The first and the last. The inward and the outward. All in the heavens and on the earth glorify God. His is the sovereignty. His is the praise.

All the beautiful names are God's. He is transcendent, immanent, hidden, evident, guardian, sovereign. To God is the destination of all.

It is wisdom, faith, reason, inspiration, and knowledge which enable man to probe and understand more and more of God's signs, the causes of things. It is by unraveling the mystery behind these signs that God can be approached and understood bit by bit. This privilege is the domain of the best of mankind-those who are engaged in expanding the frontiers of knowledge, the Nobel laureates, the galaxy of scientists, historians, archaeologists, philosophers, economists, the wise, the metaphysicians. In short, the elite of the intellectual elite. In his unceasing quest for knowledge of this world and the universe, man has just started to walk and is accelerating. **Traveling from stage to stage. 84:91**

In the words of Rumi, the Eastern poet of love and mysticism:

"A nightingale flies near the roses
A girl blushes
A pomegranate ripens
Narcissus on the edge,
Creek water washing tree roots
God is giving a general introductory lecture
We hear and read it
We will never finish reading.
Neither of us has a penny,
Yet we are walking the jeweler's bazaar

Seriously considering making a purchase!"
Reference: Translation of Rumi by Coleman Barks-"The Glance-Songs of Soul Meeting"

The distance that man has to travel on the high street of knowledge is infinite. The more man knows, the more he is aware of his ignorance, his insufficiency. Knowledge is like the circle of light caused by a burning candle, and ignorance is like the surrounding darkness. The bigger the circle of light, the bigger the corresponding circle of darkness. And the extent of God's knowledge?

Even if all the trees on earth were pens, and the ocean augmented by seven more oceans were ink,

**The words of God would not be exhausted in the writing
For God is infinitely powerful, infinitely wise. 31:27**

In the meantime, it is man's destiny to struggle and struggle. He is sure to meet God. **Forever toiling towards your Lord, painfully toiling-but you shall meet Him. 84:6** Should man misguide himself and fall by the roadside, then God **could blot him out. 84:19And God is not to be frustrated from changing man's forms and creating him in forms that he knows not. 56:60p, 61**

And now the Qura'nic authority for what has been stated and more about God.

<u>Unity of Godhead-the One and Absolute, Without Partners</u>

**He is God, one God forever Not begetting, un-begotten
And having as an equal none. 112**

And your God is one God, there is no God but He. 2:163p (2:225p, 3:2p, 3:6p, 3:18p, 2:107, and many more verses convey the same message)

God does not forgive that partners be set up with Him-but He forgives anything else...to set up partners with God is to commit a sin most serious. 4:8p

God does not forgive the sin of joining other gods with Him but forgives all else. One who joins other gods with Him has strayed far, far away. 4:116p

Those who pray to idols instead of God follow
only fancy. 10:66

Who initiates creation and then repeats it; and who provides you sustenance from the sky and the earth? Is there a deity besides God? Bring your proof if you are
being truthful. 27:64

The God other than which there is no deity: knower of the invisible and the evident, the overwhelming, the Giver of peace and safety. Glory to God beyond any association they attribute. This God, the originator, the creator, the shaper, to whom the most beautiful names belong, celebrated by everything in the heavens and on earth, being the Almighty, the Perfectly Wise. 59:23-24

There is no God but He, the creator of all things. 6:102

The order of God is coming; do not try to hasten it. Glory to God; exalted far above the partners they ascribe to Him 6:1P

Say, "Do you take to other patrons than God who cannot profit or harm themselves? Are the blind and the seeing equal? Are darkness and light equal? God is One, the Omnipotent." 13:16p

Glory to God far above the partners they ascribe to Him.
Your God is one God. 16:22 and 40:65p

And to warn those who say God has begotten a son.
They have no knowledge of this, nor had their ancestors.
What comes out of their mouths is intolerable as a maxim:
For they are only telling a lie. 18:4-5

Say "Praise be to God who begets no son.
He has no partners in His dominion." 25:2

God is the reality and whatever else they pray to is vanity. 22:62p

If there were in the heavens and the earth other deities besides God there would have been ruin in both. 21:22p and many more verses.

People of the Scripture, do not go to excess in your religion. The Messiah Jesus, son of Mary, was only a messenger.
So believe in God and God's messengers.
Do not speak of a Trinity.

God is one sole divinity too transcendent to have a son. 4:171p

"As of now, there are four fundamental forces of nature: electromagnetism, gravity, the strong force, and the weak force. Physicists are sure that the four forces are really four manifestations of a single underlying super force governing the universe. Scientists are working to unite the four forces into a single equation, a grand unifying theory-an effort to discover the primal commonality underlying the current plurality." Reference-THE CANON by Natalie Angier

If the scientists succeed, and they are bound to succeed, would the "Primal Commonality," the single equation, be the Islamic God? I have no doubt whatsoever.

Now let us look at what the latest developments in this field are. Stephen Hawking, one of the greatest thinkers and cosmological physicists says-"According to M. Theory (M. Theory is a candidate for the ultimate theory of everything. M. Theory is the only model that has all the proper properties we think the final theory ought to have. M. Theory may offer answers to the behavior of all life, but humans are conditioned) ours is not the only universe. Instead, M. Theory predicts that a great many universes were created out of nothing. Their creation does not require the intervention of some supernatural being or God. Rather, these multiple universes arise naturally from physical law. They are a prediction of science." Reference THE GRAND DESIGN, a book written by Stephen Hawking and Leonard Mlodinow and first published in 2010. The above observations about multiple universes, their creation out of nothing and in no time, gift of free will granted to man, spreading of the earth and covering it richly to serve as an abode fit for man and all life to live are in accordance with the Qura'nic observations. The **Qurán** further observes that all creation is in accordance with the law and is in a clear record. Events great or small, as small as an atom or still smaller, happen according to a blue print recorded in the Book of Nature. Everything in the universe acts according to the divine law which is immutable and eternal. The **Qurán** further states:

A. The heavens and the earth and all that is between them have been created in due proportion and for a definite term.

B. The beginning of time and its end is coeval with the birth and the end of the universe.

C. Everything has been created in pairs. Please see Chapter 15 for the Qura'nic authority.

Islamic God is Universal

The Islamic God is the God of the universe, of all mankind. He is not the God of a nation, a race, a sect, a cult, or of any one religion.

God, Lord of all the worlds 1:2p

God is full of bounty to mankind. 2:243p
God is full of bounty to all the worlds.   2:251p
God cares for all. 2:68p
God, the Cherisher and Sustainer of the worlds. 7:54p
Whatever God out of mercy, bestows on mankind,
None can withhold. 35:2p
Lord of the heavens and of the earth and all between them
And Lord of every point at the rising of the sun. 37:5
God! Lord of all the worlds. 40:64p
Cherisher of all the worlds.   45:36p
The God of humankind.   114:3
Lord of the heavens and the earth and all that is in between. 38:66
Praise is proper to God, the Cherisher and Sustainer of the worlds. 1:1
The Supporter of all 3:2p
O mankind fear your guardian Lord. 4:1p

Note: **Qurán** mentions many more verses emphasizing God's universality.

God the Creator

Creation is God's major activity. Every moment millions of creatures die and millions are born. The universe is in flux perpetually. It was created from a void and for a definite term.

God is the creator of all things. 13:6
This is God the creator, the originator. 59:24
God created man from water. 25:54p
We created the human beings from an extract of earth. 23:12

It is God who created the heavens and the earth by truth, the day God says 'Be' then it is. 6:73p (The Big Bang?)

Or isn't the One who created the heavens and the earth, able to create their like? Certainly, being the absolute Creator. 36:81

It is God who created for you all that is on earth, then turned to the firmaments and proportioned them into seven heavens. 2:29

Do not you see that God created the heavens and the earth in truth? If God willed, God would remove you and bring a new generation. 14:19 and 4:133

God has created the heavens and the earth in just proportions and formed you, fashioned you expertly, and the destination is to God. 64:3

We did not create the heavens and the earth and everything in between in jest: We created them for just ends but most of them do not know. 44:38-39

God created the heavens and the earth with justice, that every soul be requited for what it earned, without being wronged. 45:22

Creator of the heavens from nothingness, who on having determined something, simply says to it 'Be' and it is.
2:117 and 40:68

Then God designed the sky which had been vapor. 41:11p

We have not created the heavens and the earth and all that is between them but in due proportion and for a definite term. 46:3p

God creates what He wills. 3:40p and 22:14p, 22:18, 3:47, 14:27p

We have created pairs of everything so that you may contemplate. 51:49

The Most Gracious created man, taught him intelligent speech. 51:4

God is the One who created seven heavens and as many earths, with the order descending among them. 65:12p

God created the seven heavens in correspondence; you see no disharmony in the creation of the Most Gracious. Now look: do you see any flaw? Turn your vision again and again. Your gaze comes back dazed and weary. 6:7

And God created all animals from water and God creates what He wills. 24:45p

Glorify the name of your Lord, the Highest, who has created, and given order and proportion, Who has ordained laws and granted guidance. 87:1-3

God created the sun, the moon, and stars subject to the divine order. Are creation and order not up to God? 7:54p

God is Indefinable, Unique, Supreme, Immanent, Transcendent, Beyond Comprehension

Everyone has an aim to which God gives directions; so strive in everything good. Wherever you are, God will bring you together. 2:148p

When my servants ask you about Me, I'm close indeed-I listen to the prayer of the supplicant when one calls on Me. 2:186p

No vision comprehends God, but God comprehends all vision. 6:103p

God is beyond what they describe. 21:22p

Glory to God, transcendent beyond what they assert. 37:159

They have not truly assessed the measure of God. God is transcendent beyond any association they make. 39:67p

Everything in the heavens and the earth glorifies God, the first and the last,
The outward and the inward. 57:2-3

The status of our Lord is transcendent
Admitting of neither mate nor offspring. 72:3p

Lord of power, transcending whatever they describe. 37:180

This is God, other than which there is no deity: knower of the invisible and the evident, the overwhelming, the giver of peace and safety. Glory to God beyond any association they attribute. 59:22-23

God is beyond anything they describe, knowing the hidden and the manifest, transcendent beyond any association they impute. 23:91-2 see also 10:18

Glory to your Lord, Lord of Power,
Transcending whatever they describe. 37:180

There is none like Him. 42:11p

He is irresistibly supreme over all things. 6:18p also 6:61p
Every day He shines in new splendor. 55:29p

Say, "Call upon God or call upon All-Rehman, by whatever name you call upon Him it is well, for to Him belong the most beautiful names." 17:110p and 20:8

God created the heavens and the earth and
All between them in six days then mounted the throne of authority. 32:4p

God rules all affairs from the heavens to the earth:
In the end all affairs go up to Him,
On a day that will last a thousand years of your reckoning. 32:5

All affairs are referred to God. 35:4P

Every creature in the heavens and on earth seeks its needs from God. 59:27p

<u>Omnipotent, Omniscient, Sovereign, Wise, and Ultimate in Knowledge</u>

Whatever is in the heavens and on earth belongs to God and God has power over all things. 2:84p

Say, "O, my God, possessor of all powers, you have the power over all things." 3:26p and 3:189

The power over the heavens and the earth and what is in between them is God's; and God is capable of everything. 5:150

God is mighty, powerful. 13:13p

All there is in the heavens and the earth glorifies God. His is the Sovereignty and His is the praise; and He has power over everything. 64:1

Doer of what all He intends. 85:16

Blessed is the one Who holds the dominion
And Who has power over all things. 67:1

To Whom belong the sovereignty of the heaven and the earth and God is witness to everything. 85:9

Indeed, nothing is hidden from God on earth or in the heavens. 3:5

Say, "Whether you conceal what is in your heart or reveal it, God knows it and God knows what is in heaven and what is on earth and God is capable of all things." 3:29 also 5:97p

By the Knower of the unknown-from whom not so much as a particle escapes notice in the heavens or on earth; and there is nothing smaller than that or larger but is in a clear record. 34:3p

God does what He plans. 11:107p

And of all things, He has perfect knowledge. 2:29

Then know that God is all-powerful, all-wise. 2:209p

God is the One Who hears and knows all things. 2:224p

God is full of knowledge and power. 49:50p

God, the Omniscient. 36:81p

God the Omnipotent. 65:12p

It is God Who has the knowledge of the end of time and who
showers the rain,
And Who knows what is in the wombs.
No soul knows what it will earn tomorrow,
And no soul knows in what land it will die:
But God is omniscient, completely aware. 31:34

And God created all animals from water:
Some of them travel on their bellies,
Some travel on two legs, some travel on four.
God creates what God wills; God is capable of all things. 24:45

God sees and hears all things. 31:28

He is God. There is no God but He

The knower of the hidden and the evident. 6:73p

Note: More than 200 verses mention these aspects.

<u>Beginning and End of All Things-All Go Back to God</u>

All affairs wind up with God. 42:53p

The final goal is to your Lord. 53:42

All matters derive from God and return to God. 3:109p and 8:44p

It is to God that you return, all of you. 10:4p and 96:8

**God brings life and deals death and to God you will be returned.
10:56**

The secret of the heavens and the earth
Belong to God, to whom everything is returned. 11:123p

God knows what is before them and what is behind them;
And all affairs are referred to God. 22:76 and 35:4p

To Me is the destination of all. 22:48

To God belongs the judgment-to God you will be returned. 28:70p

Sustainer, Protector, Helper, and Cherisher of the Worlds, Benevolent, Beneficent, Kind, Compassionate, Merciful, Forbearing, and Bountiful

God! The Cherisher and Sustainer of the worlds 1:2p and 10:10, 7:54p

The Lord and Cherisher of the universe 2:131p and 5:28, 6:45p, 6:162p and many others

God is the protector of believers. 2:257p

But God is your protector and God is the best of Helpers. 3:150

God is sufficient as a protector and God is sufficient as a helper. 4:5p

God is a friend and a helper. 9:116p also 10:57, 20:60, 42:28p, 51:58, 89:15 and more

All but one of the hundred and fourteen chapters of the **Qurán** open with the words **In the name of God, the compassionate the caring.**

This verse has also been translated as:

In the name of God, the beneficent, the merciful.
In the name of God most gracious, most merciful.
In the name of God, most gracious, the Dispenser of grace.

This invocation is uttered many times by every Muslim in his daily living. These are the aspects most mentioned in the **Qurán** and represent the overwhelming qualities of God.

God is most forgiving, most merciful. 2:218p

These qualities find mention in more than fifty verses.

God is supporter of all. 2:225p and 3:2p

God cares for all. 2:261p and 2:268p

He is most forbearing. 2:263p

God is the Lord of bounties unbounded. 3:174p

But your God is forgiving, full of benevolence. 18:58p

Indeed He is compassionate and kind. 2:37p and 2:163

God is forgiving and kind. 2:173p and twenty more verses

Indeed God bestows His blessings on men. 2:243

But God is full of bounty to all the worlds. 2:251p

The Mighty and the Merciful. 32:6p

The benevolent One has raised the sky and set the balance. 55:7

God, the benevolent, ever merciful. 59:22p, 55:1

Every creature in the heavens and on earth seeks its needs from God. 59:29p

Your Lord is swift in punishment and yet is truly forgiving and merciful. 6:165p

To everyone We give, to this one and that one, from the gift of your Lord. And the gift of your Lord is not restricted. 17:20

Read for your Lord is most generous. 96:3

It is God who accepts repentance from His servants and forgives sins. 42:25p

Your Lord is uniquely independent and yet merciful. 6:133p

Relate to My devotees who have transgressed against their own souls! Do not despair of God's mercy for God forgives all sins! Indeed, God is the epitome of forgiveness and mercy. 39:53

To those who avoid sins and vile acts, discounting minor offenses, your Lord is indeed extensive in forgiving. 53:32p

God is truly kind and merciful to humanity. 22:65p

God acts on divine will 2:53

Verily, God does what He plans. 11:107p and 85:16

Giver of Life and Death

Your Lord is the giver of life and death. 2:58p

It is God that gives life and death. 3:156p, 23:80p, 53:44

There is no other deity than the One Who gives life and causes death. 7:158p

God gives life and causes death and you have no protector and no Savior aside from God. 9:116

God is Free of All Needs

And if any strive, they do so for their own souls for God is independent of the creatures of all the worlds. 29:6

God is free of all wants. 226:3, 2:267p, 41:31p, 31:26p

God, the Law Giver, God's Law is Immutable, Eternal

Do not you know that God knows what is in heaven and on earth? For that is in a decree. 22:70p
O society of Jinns and men: cross the bounds of heaven and the earth, if you have the ability then pass beyond them; but you cannot unless you acquire the law. 55:33

The sun and the moon follow courses exactly compounded. 55:5

Neither the sun can overtake the moon nor the night outpace the day. Each swims along in its orbit according to law. 36:40

Extol the name of your Guardian Lord, the Highest Who has created and
Further given order and proportion,
Who has ordained laws and granted guidance. 87:1,2,3

You will find no change in Our Law. 17:77p

No change will you find in the law of God. 33:62p

No change will you find in God's Law.
Nor will you find Divine law mutable. 35:43p
Such has been the Law of God in the past.
No change will you find in the Law of God. 48:23

None can challenge the word of God. 6:115

Extent of God's Knowledge

Even if all the trees on earth were pens,
And the ocean augmented by seven more oceans were ink
The words of God would not be exhausted in the writing
For God is infinitely powerful, infinitely wise. 31:27

Even if the ocean were ink for the words of My Lord
The ocean would be exhausted
Before the words of My Lord were exhausted,
Even if We brought another ocean for its aid. 18:109

Reality

God is the Reality and all else is vanity. 22:62p

God is the only Reality and whatever else
They invoke besides Him is falsehood 31:30p

The Light

God is the light of the heavens and the earth
The likeness of divine light is as of a niche with a lamp inside.
The lamp enclosed in glass, the glass as it were a brilliant star.
Lit from a blessed Tree, an Olive, neither of the East nor of the West
Whose Oil is well-nigh luminous.
Though fire scarce touched it, light upon Light!
God guides whom He will to His Light,
God does set forth Parables for men; and God knows all things.
24:35

(Lit is such a Light)in houses, which God has permitted to be raised to honor;
For the celebration in them, of His name:
In them is He glorified in the mornings
And in the evenings (again and again.) 24:36

They wish to extinguish the light of God with their words,
But God insists on fulfilling the divine light
Even if the disbelievers are averse. 9:32

They want to extinguish the light of God with their mouths
But God will complete the divine illumination
In spite of the hatred of the atheists. 61:8

God is the Truth

The truth is from your Lord. So be not at all in doubt. 2:147

High above all is God...The Truth. 20:144p

The word of God is the Truth. 6:73p

The word of your Lord is fulfilled in truth and justice. 10:32p

Islamic Philosophy of Reward and Punishment

All through human history, all societies, tribes, faiths, nations etc. have specified do's and don'ts for its members. There is reward for the observant and punishment for the deviant. The notion of life after death and heaven and hell were prevalent in the earliest human civilizations as well. Simultaneously, deities were conceived as the power who enforced these rewards and punishments. The monarch, the conqueror, the tribal chief, or the religious leader including the witch doctor, were the deities' representatives on earth and acted as the supreme enforcer of the values specified as good or evil.

Islam also has its concept of good and evil, of life after death, of heaven and hell, and of a Deity. The nature of the Islamic God has been discussed in this chapter. The rewards and punishments are of two types, one in this world, and the other in the life to come. Rewards and punishments in this world are clear. **Qurán** is a book of guidance. The way of God is the straight way, the way of the law. If you breach the law you suffer the consequences in this world, if you observe it, you taste the reward in this world. The law is universal-applicable to all of mankind.

Now for the life to come. Paradise is the reward for the good, and hell the destination of the sinners.

<u>Paradise Defined</u>

The garden of perpetual bliss. 9:72 and a few more
The garden of rest and promise. 32:19
Home of peace, in the presence of their Lord. 6:127p
A home that will last; without toil and without weariness. 35:35

For those who fear God are mansions built with lofty chambers above and rivers running below. 39:20p

For those who have rightly acted is happiness and more:
No dust will cover their faces, and no ignominy
They are the company of the Garden where they all abide. 10:26

The eternal garden promised to the righteous, a reward as well as a goal. 25:15
God will preserve them from the adverse effects of that day,
Imbuing them with health and happiness;
And reward them for their constancy with the garden and silk
They will recline on couches there in seeing neither sun nor frost.
And bunches of grapes will hang low,

And vessels of silver will be passed around among them,
And cups of glass, of silvery glass and they will be given a cup to
drink
Of a blend of ginger, of a spring called delectable.
And they will be surrounded with immortalized children, like
strewn pearls
And when you look you would see happiness, a magnificent
dominion.
Covering them will be clothing of silk brocade, green and glittering,
And they will be adorned with silver bracelets.
This is a reward for you, as your effort is appreciated. 76:11-22

As for the conscientious, they will be in gardens with streams,
In the seat of truth in the presence of an omnipotent sovereign.
54:54-55

For the sincere servants of God: there is a determined provision,
Fruits; and they will be honored in gardens of felicity
On divans facing each other
While a cup from a fountain is passed around to them,
Pure water, a delight to those who drink, with no intoxication in it
And with them there will be demure women with large eyes,
Delicate, chaste. 37:42, 49

For the conscientious there will be an abode of felicity. 78:31

There will be no nonsense there, and no falsehood. 78:35

As for the conscientious, they will be in a secure abode
Amidst gardens and springs, wearing silk and brocade, facing one
another
We will pair them with doe-eyed maidens,
There they can call for every fruit in peace, they will not taste death
there,
Except the first death as a blessing from your Lord.
That is the great salvation. 44:51-6p and 57

And paradise will be brought near the conscientious. 50:31p

Enter there in peace. That is the day of eternity.
They will have what they wish there,
And a super abundance in our presence. 50:34-35

An agreeable life, in lofty gardens where fruits are at hand
Eat and drink with pleasure, for you have earned it in days gone
by. 69:21-24

They will be the favorite sin gardens of happiness
On couches inlaid with gold and jewels, reclining on them,
Facing each other surrounded by immortalized children
With goblets and jugs and cups from fountains
And there will be food for them to choose from
And whatever flesh of fowl they desire
And there will be large-eyed maidens like treasured pearls,
As a reward for what they did
There will hear no nonsense there and no opposition-
Only the saying, Peace, peace! 56:11-12, 15-18, 20-26

They will be amidst lotus trees without thorns
And orderly acacias with extensive shade and flowing water
And abundant fruit which is never unavailable and never out of
season;
And high cushions. We have created the females as a special creation,
Making them virgins, loving wives as companions
For the company of the right. 56:28-38

Two gardens in lush profusion, in each of them two springs flowing
Fruits in pairs of every kind the fruit bending near; dates and
pomegranates
Among them beauties with shy glances like ruby and coral
Undeflowered by human or jinn, reclining on carpets with silken
Interior and gold brocade. In them are women good and fair
Eyes deep black flashing white, shy eyes sheltered in pavilions.
55:46-76

(only those verses defining paradise have been selected)

The Deserving of Paradise

My mercy extends to all things
Those who are conscientious and pay welfare tax regularly.
And those who believe in our signs. 7:156p

Those who believe and do good works and humbly submit to their
Lord,
They are the company of paradise where they will abide. 11:23
Who persevere in seeking the way of the Lord
Who fulfill their devotional obligations,
And spent what we have given them secretly or openly,
Who repel evil with good, for them is the reward of paradise. 13:22

Those who are conscientious,
For those who have done good in this world
There is good and the home of the hereafter is better still.
How excellent is the home of the conscientious, everlasting gardens.
16:30-31p

As for those who believe and did good works,
There are the gardens of the paradise as a welcome. 18:107
Those were some of the prophets whom God graced
From the descendants of Adam,
And from those We carried along with Noah,
And from the offspring of Abraham and Israel,
From among those We guided and chose,
Whenever the signs of the benevolent one
Were related to them, they would fall down, prostrate and weeping
But a generation came after them
Who neglected prayer and followed earthly pleasures
They will reach the wrong road and meet perdition
Except those who repent and believe and work righteousness,
Everlasting gardens, which the Benevolent
Has promised to the devotees, in the unseen future:
For His promise must come to pass. 19:58-59,61p

And for those who believe and do good deeds We will prepare for them Lofty dwellings in the garden, a perfect reward for those who toil. 29:58
Who are constant in their prayers
And those in whose wealth is an acknowledged right
For the poor and the outcast,
Those who recognize the reality of the Day of Judgment.

70:23, 26

Those who respect their pledges and promises
Those who stand by their testimonies
And those who are mindful of their prayers
They will be honored in the gardens. 71:32-35

As for the upright, they will drink from a cup of a blend of camphor.
They fulfill woes, and they feed, for love of God
The poor, the orphan, and the captive:
We are feeding solely for the sake of God;
We want no compensation from you, not even thanks. 76:5,7p, 8-9

As for the conscientious, they will be in gardens with streams,
In the seat of truth In the presence of an omnipotent sovereign.
54:54-55

This is a reminder; for there is a beautiful resort for the conscientious:
Eternal gardens, whose doors are open to them;
Where they may recline, where they may call
For fruit in abundance, and drink;
And with them will be demure females of the same age. 38:49-52
For the conscientious, here will be an abode of felicity
They will hear no nonsense there, and no falsehood
A deserved gift from your Lord. 78:31, 35,36p

Those who give of their wealth night and day, secretly and openly,
Have their reward with their Lord;
And no fear will weigh on them, and they will not sorrow. 2:274
As for those who believe and do good works
And pray regularly and give charity,
They have their reward with their Lord;

And no fear will weigh on them, and they will not sorrow. 2:277

Those who believe and do good works and humbly acquiesce to
their Lord,
They are the company of paradise, where they will abide. 11:23

Who persevere in seeking the countenance of the Lord
Who fulfill their devotional obligations, and spend what we have
given them
Secretly or openly, who repel evil with good
For them is the reward of paradise. 13:22p

The words 'righteousness' and 'conscientious' carry the same
meaning and have been used many times in the above verses. The
Qura'nic definition is:

Righteousness is not that you should turn
Your faces to the east and the west;
Rather, the righteous are those who believe in God and the last day,
And the angels and scriptures and prophets;
And who give material gifts out of love for God,
Even if what they care for, to relatives and orphans,
And the poor and the traveler and the needy,
And for the purpose of liberating the enslaved;
And who pray regularly and give alms;
And who fulfill their promises when they promise;
And those who are patient in misfortune, affliction, and hard times;
They are the ones who confirm the truth, and they are the
conscientious. 2:177
Is the reward for good anything but good? 55:60

Hell Defined

A miserable place to rest. 2:206p
A miserable destination. 3:162p
A miserable bed. 3:12p

We have prepared a fire for the unjust,
Whose billowing smoke will envelop them.

And if they pray for rain, we will rain on them water like molten brass,
That will burn their faces. What a miserable drink,
And what a terrible place to rest. 18:29p

Seize him and bind him, and let him burn in the blaze.
Then make him walk in a chain 70 cubits long. 69:30-32

As for hell, it is an ambush, a destination for oppressors
Where they will remain for eons.
They will taste nothing cool there, and no drink but boiling and putrid. 78:21-26

So have a taste, for We will not give you more of anything but agony. 78:30

Have you heard tell of the calamity? Some faces will be downcast that day,
Laboring, exhausted, roasting in a burning fire,
Given drink from a boiling spring. There will be no food for them
But bitter tarn that neither nourishes nor satisfies hunger. 88:1-7
Those whose balance is slight, wind up in an abyss.
And what will convey to you what this is? Raging fire. 101:8-11

The most wretched will turn away-Those who will roast in the greatest fire
Where they will neither die nor live. 87:11-13

The deviants will be in a blaze, where they will roast on the day of requital,
Unable to hide from it
And what will let you know what the day of requital is?
The day no soul can do anything for another;
For the matter is up to God. 82:14-19

Scorching wind and boiling water, and the shadows of black smoke,
Without refreshment, without hospitality. 56:42-44

Deserving of Hell

Woe to every back biting critic who gathers money and multiplies it
Assuming his wealth will make him last.
But no, he will be flung into destruction. 104:1-4

As for those who disbelieved, among both
People of scripture and polytheists,
They will be in hell fire, where they will remain.
They are the worst of creation. 98:6
Those who repudiate our signs we will burn them in a fire. 4:56p
As for those who are stingy and complacent
We will facilitate hardship for them.
And their wealth won't help them when they fall. 92:8, 10-11

Where none will roast but the most wretched,
Those who deny truth and turn away. 92:14-15

Woe to the cheaters who demand full measure
When they receive from people
But short them when they measure or weigh for them
Don't they think they will be resurrected for a trying day?
The day when humankind will stand before the Lord of the
Universe?
As for the destiny of the deviants,
They will be in a prison. And what is prison? A sealed fate.
Woe to the unbelievers on that day who deny the reality of the day
of requital
Which none deny but an aggressive sinner
When our signs are read to him calls them myths of the ancients
By no means they will be shut out from their Lord
And they will be roasting in hell
And they will be told this is what you used to deny. 83:1-17
He did not believe in almighty God and did not encourage feeding
the poor.
So he has no friend here today and no food but puss
Which no one eats but those in error. 69:23-27

On the day when some faces will be black and gloomy
They will be asked "Did you reject faith after accepting it?"
Taste then the penalty for rejecting faith. 3:106p

They had been granted the good things in life before that,
Yet they persisted in terrible things. And they used to say what?
When we have died and become dust and bones,
Will we really be resurrected?'
They will be gathered together for the deadline of a determined day
Then you will-you who are confused, imputing falsehood to truth-
You will eat of a bitter tree, filling your guts from it,
And drinking boiling water on top of that. 56:45-47, 50-54

As for those who repudiated our signs and considered themselves
above them,
The doors of heaven will not be opened to them
For them is a bed of hell with coverings of fire over them
That is how we reward wrong doers. 7:40p, 41

God is Just and Takes Account

And none shall be dealt with unjustly on the Day of Judgment.
2:281
God does not place on a soul a burden greater than it can bear.
One gets what one has earned and suffers every evil that it earns.
2:286p

These are the signs of God which we declare to you in truth,
And God does not wish in justice to any of His creatures. 3:108

That is for what you did for yourself
For God never does injustice to his devotees
If there is any good God redoubles it and gives a magnificent reward
From the divine presence. 4:40

So follow the inspiration revealed to you,
And be patient until God renders Judgment,
For God is the best of judges. 10:103
Is not God the wisest of Judges? 95:8

Your Lord is not the one to strike down unjustly. 11:117p
Your Lord will requite them all fully. 11:111

God created the heavens and the earth with justice,
That every soul be requited for what it earned without being wrong ed. 45:22
And there are degrees for everyone, according to what they have done,
As recompense for their deeds; and no injustice will be done to them. 46:19
Those who repudiate our signs we will burn them in a fire
So they can taste the torment. For God is most powerful, most judicious. 4:56
Indeed God is mighty, the Lord of retribution. 14:47p
You Lord is full of forgiveness for mankind for their errors.
But your Lord is also strict in punishment. 13:6p
But the unbelievers-their deeds are like a mirage in sandy deserts,
Which the thirsty mistake for water until he reaches it and finds nothing there,
Though he finds God with him who pays him his due
And God is swift in accounting. 24:39
Yet among the people are those who take to idols instead of God;
When they see the punishment
They will see that God is severe in punishment. 2:165p
These will be allotted what they have earned;
And God is quick in account. 2:202see also 14:51
Whoever rejects the signs of God, Surely God is quick to take account. 3:19p
And you will surely be questioned about what you have been doing. 16:93p
That day they will hear a blast in truth
That will be the day of resurrection. 50:42

The verdict about who goes to heaven and hell comes on the Day of Judgment.

We shall set up scales of justice for the Day of Judgment,
So that not a soul will be dealt with unjustly in the least.
And if there be no more than the weight of a mustard seed,

We will bring it to account. And enough are We to take account. 21:47

<u>The Day of Judgment Defined</u>

Like the Qura'nic description of God or heaven or hell, the description of the Day of Judgment is intense, powerful, and evocative.

The Day of Judgment has been given many names:

1. The Momentous Event (69:1)
2. The Day of Requital (56:56)
3. The Day of Resurrection or the Day of Judgment (2:8)
4. The Day of Testimony (11:03p)
5. The Gathering Together (11:103p)
6. The End of Time(45:27) or The Last Day (2:8, 65 etc.)
7. The Inevitable (56:1)
8. The Day of Noise and Clamor (101:1)
9. The Day of Accountability or Reckoning (38:16, 26)
10. The Day of Assembly (42:7)
11. The Hour(7:187)
12. The Overwhelming Event (79:34)
13. The Promised Day (50:20)
14. The Day of Ultimate Truth (78:39)
15. A Determined Day (56:50)
16. The Day of God (14:26)
17. Day of Decision (32:29)
18. Day of Regrets (19:39)
19. Day of Loss and Gain (64:9)
20. The Day of Distress (25:26)

These names also define the Day of Judgment.

God, master of the Day of Judgment. 1:4
God will certainly gather you together on the Day of Judgment
About which there is no doubt. 4:87p

That is a day for which mankind will be gathered together:
That will be a day of testimony. 11:103p

And every one of them will come to Him singly on the Day of
Judgment. 19:95
Say, "God gives you life, and then makes you die,
And then gathers you for the day of accountability
About which there is no doubt; but most people do not know
And the day on which the end of time will happen,
The liars will lose out and you will see every nation kneeling;
Every nation will be summoned to its record:
Today you are being repaid for what you did." 45:26, 27p 28

The earth will split asunder. They will come out hurriedly.
This gathering is easy for us. 50:44

When the inevitable comes to pass there will be none who deny its
happening
Humbling and exalting when the earth is shaken with a shock
And the mountains are crushed into scattered dust. 56:1-6

The momentous event. What is the momentous event?
When the trumpet is sounded once, and the earth is picked up,
Mountains and all, and they are demolished, crushed all at once
On that day the inevitable will come to pass:
The sky will be split apart, for it will be fragile that day
On that day you will be exposed;
No secret of yours will be hidden. 69:1-2, 4-5, 6-7, 9

The day when the sky will be like molten brass,
And the mountains will be like shredded wool
And a friend won't ask after a friend, even though they see them
The sinner will wish he could bail himself out of the agony of
that day
By sacrificing his children, and his wife, and his brother,
And his family sheltering him, and everyone on earth, in order to
save him
By no means? For that is raging fire pulling insistently by the scalp.
70:8-16

When the sun is rolled up, when the stars fall lusterless
When the mountains are blown away, when the pregnant camels
are neglected
When the wild beasts are herded, when the oceans are flooded
When the souls are matched
When the infant girl who was buried is asked for what offense was
she killed:
When the pages are opened, when the sky is stripped,
When the blaze is fired up, when the garden is drawn near
Each soul will know what is has brought about. 81:1-14

When the sky splits and when the stars are scattered
And when the oceans are drained and when the tombs are upset,
Each soul will know what it produced and what it left undone.
82:1-5

And what will let you know what the day of requital is? 82:17
The day no soul can do anything for another:
For the matter that day is up to God. 82:19

Beyond the Day of Judgment

There are two more dimensions which need to be mentioned here. One
is the extent of the reward for the good and punishment for the guilty,
and the other, the Divine forgiveness.

Extent of Reward

If there is any good, God redoubles it
And gives a magnificent reward from the divine presence. 4:40p

God may reward mankind for the best of what they did,
And even grant them more, out of the divine bounty
And God provides for whomever He will beyond accounting.
24:38p
Those who give of their wealth in the way of God
Are like grain that sprouts seven ears with a hundred kernels in
each ear.
And God may choose to multiply what anyone has at will. 2:261p

Extent of Punishment

He that does evil shall only be recompensed according to his evil,
No wrong shall be done to him. 6:160p

In the scales of justice set up on the Day of Judgment, the reward for good deeds is multiplied many, many times and God further adds to the reward from His bounty. The other scale carries only the punishment according to the evil done. There is therefore no doubt what so ever that the scale of reward will always weigh heavier than the other scale. This will be true for the vast majority of mankind, if not all. Then comes God's mercy and forgiveness.

If you avoid the worst of what you are forbidden,
We will efface your evil from you and lead you to a place of honor.
4:31
To those who avoid serious sins and wild acts,
Your Lord is indeed extensive in forgiveness. 53:32
And those who remember God and the one who brings the truth,
And the one who confirms it, they are the conscientious
They will have whatever they wish in the presence of their Lord
That is the reward of those who do good
That God may pardon the worst of their deeds,
And reward them for the best of what they used to do.

39:33-35

God is ever pardoning. 4:149p
To everyone We give, to this one and that one from the gift of your
Lord.
And the gift of your Lord is not restricted. 17:20
What are serious sins?
God does not forgive idolatry, but forgives anything else. 4:48p

Those who accept the faith then disbelieve
Then return to it and deny once again and increase in disbelief
Will not be forgiven by God or be guided by Him. 4:137

In the end, God's mercy extends to polytheists, atheists, and apostates as well.

Relate O my devotees who have transgressed against their own souls
Do not despair of God's mercy, for God forgives all sins.
Indeed God is epitome of forgiveness and mercy. 39:53
O, soul in repose, return to your Lord, pleased and accepted,
Join the company of my servants, enter into My Garden. 89:27-30

It is crystal clear that, at the end of the day, all stand forgiven by God, most merciful, most forgiving.

It is probably for this reason that paradise is a "sign" word.

Be quick in the race for forgiveness from your Lord.
And for a Garden as wide as the entire heavens and the earth.
3:133p

If the Garden and the universe are co-equal, one could well wonder where is the room for hell? Does it mean that heaven and hell have no existence? In any case, these symbols of reward and punishment take effect only after the Day of Judgment when mankind has been judged and classified. But the judgment day is also the end of time. Does anything survive time? Not a probability. In any case, as the **Qurán** states, after the catastrophe also known as the Day of Calamity, the universe lapses into void, a nothingness, taking with it heaven and hell also. In the initial creation, the universe was created from nothingness (2:117p) and for a definite period of time. (46:3p)

End of time also suggests a beginning of time. Such are the mysteries God sets for mankind to probe and unravel.

If everyone is forgiven at the end of the day where is the justification for this elaborate system of carrots and sticks? One reason probably is the limitation of human institutions to detect and punish all sins. This inability is more pronounced in the domain of morality. How do you keep mankind away from evil and what appears to be gross injustice of which there is no dirth of in this world? By extending this world into the next where the simple human urge for justice and peace and plenty is assured; where man lives without struggle, without fear of death, without evil? Always in the presence of God's grace. In short, the Utopia, the Arcadia, the wished for ideal in this world. Or is it a pointer for creating heaven on earth? I must hasten to clarify that these are conjectures based on the knowledge of **Qurán**. The final resolution of it all must wait for human knowledge to increase until it is able to solve these mysteries.

Here I am reminded of an incident that happened to me and my younger brother in childhood and which has left a permanent impression on us. Once, my mother saw us teasing baby frogs and killing one of them. She was furious and warned us that if we take life, any life that is not a danger to us, our children will be born deaf and dumb. That is God's punishment for sure. This terrified us and was very effective. When we grew up we knew that it was not true, and we yet passed on this story to our children and their children.

<u>Conclusion</u>

Fine so far. But then what is the primary message of the **Qurán**, the purpose of its revelation? The focus is on this world. Islam consists of three major components:

1. <u>Faith</u>-Faith is a personal matter. If a person affirms faith as defined in verses 2:1-5, none is given the right to question that faith.
2. <u>Rites and Rituals</u>-Fasting, prayers, Haj (pilgrimage to Mecca) A believer performs these rituals for his own benefit, spiritually and to be a fit and responsible member of the Muslim community. God is self-sufficient, independent of His creatures, and beyond any need of human supplications.
3. <u>Islamic Polity</u>-To establish an Islamic social system. The important pillars of this system are:
   a. acquiring knowledge (Chapter 4)
   b. freedom from poverty and want (Chapter 5)
   c. respect for members of all faiths, creeds, etc. and brotherhood (Chapter 6)
   d. justice according to law (Chapter 10)
   e. equal status for men and women (Chapter 8)

Qura'nic pronouncements on these and a few other areas including economics, history, environment, and genesis and evolution of man have been brought out in this book. All these are mundane issues. There are many more which do not form part of this book and yet are germane to life on earth. These draw man's attention to the primacy of establishing paradise on earth. Straying communities invite God's wrath played out on this earth. It goes without saying that Muslim communities are the victims of God's displeasure at this moment of time in history. The baton is in the hands of nations following His guidance, His directives.

These aspects are beyond the ken of Muslim clerics. Their focus is on life after death. If they want a renaissance of Islam, they will have to change direction, unfreeze the Book, open the door for ijtihad, (independent reasoning) in the interpretation of the **Qurán** and seek guidance exclusively from the divine message and concentrate on this world.

But seek the abode of the hereafter with what God has bestowed on you,
And do not forget your part in this world.
And be good, as God has been good to you.
And do not seek corruption on earth for God does not love the corrupt. 28:77
Whoever desires the reward in this world, We grant him.
And whoever desires the reward in the hereafter
We grant him. And We will swiftly reward the grateful.
And those who believe with the enduring Word they will be established in the life of this world and in the hereafter. 3:145p and 14:27p

In conclusion, kindly pause and ponder over this verse.

O Soul in repose, return to your Lord, pleased and accepted.
Join the company of My servants, enter into My heaven. 89:27-30

It is the soul that enters heaven and reposes in the shadow of God's grace, not the gross body which perishes.

Chapter Three

MUHAMMAD (P.B.U.H)

I am only a man like you.
A messenger from God.
Reciting immaculate pages
In which are just decrees. 98:23
Rehearsing God's signs to you,
Purifies you and instructs you in Scripture and wisdom and
in new knowledge. 2:151

It is not in my power to harm you or bring you to right conduct.
72:21
I am not the disposer of your affairs.   42:6p

Chapter 3

Mission of Muhammad (P.B.U.H)

Muhammad,(P.B.U.H)* meaning the praised, messenger of God, the perfect man, according to Muslims (A PROPHET FOR OUR TIME, according to Karen Armstrong) was born about 600 years after Jesus Christ (P.B.U.H) another prophet of God. Like Moses, David, and Jesus, Muhammad was also vouchsafed a book, the **Qurán**. Muhammad(570-632CE) was born in Mecca, an important trading and religious center of Arabia, located in the West central coast of the peninsula, not far from the Red Sea. He was a scion of a noble family of the tribe of Quraish which enjoyed high precedence and respect in the tribal hierarchy. His father Abdullah died before he was born. He lost his mother Amina when he was only about six years of age. He was later brought up in loving care first by his grandfather and after his death, by an uncle. In this phase of life, Muhammad fell on difficult times, financially. This phase however ended at the age of about twenty-five when he married Khadijah, a rich merchant widow, his senior in age and a distant relative. The marriage brought him financial independence and a loving and caring companion.

The people of Mecca and the surrounding areas were predominantly polytheists. They believed neither in the life after death nor in the Day of Judgment. For them the earthly life was the beginning and the end. Theirs was a tribal society. The tribal leader was chosen by the

---

* The abbreviation p.b.u.h stands for "peace be upon him." This is a short prayer that Muslims invoke invariably while naming the prophets of God. **Qurán** mentions twenty-five prophets, including Abraham (P.B.U.H), Moses (P.B.U.H), and Jesus (P.B.U.H).

tribe. Important issues were decided by the tribal chief after consulting prominent members of the tribe. Life in the desert was harsh and ruthless.

Water and food for men and animals were scarce. This led to frequent conflicts between tribes. Travel in the desert was a nightmare. There was only one path where waterholes lay buried that would take you to your destination. If you strayed, you were dead. **Qurán** describes this situation thus: **The deeds of the unbelievers are like a mirage in sandy deserts which the man parched with thirst mistakes for water until he reaches it and finds nothing there: though he finds God with him Who pays him his due. 24:30p**

It was the responsibility of the tribal community to take care of the poor, the widow, and the orphan in their tribe. The Arabs were hospitable, kept their word and were eloquent in speech. Poetry, horses, and camels were the objects of their love and attention. They were endowed with excellent memories. In Mecca the Kabah, a cube shaped granite shrine was the center of religious devotion. It was the sanctuary of innumerable idols, stone carvings or likenesses of their objects of devotion placed by their followers living in Mecca and the surrounding areas. An image of Jesus Christ also adorned this gallery of deities. This tradition of respect and accommodation of all faiths is also a distinctive feature of Islam.

The city of Mecca was also an important trading center. Each year the tribes from all over central Arabia gathered there to trade and worship. This was also an occasion for many festive, cultural, and sporting events such as recitation of poetry and horse and camel racing etc. This gathering lasted for three to four months and brought many economic benefits to the people of Mecca. Fighting, quarrelling, and killing etc. around Kabah, the sacred precinct, were forbidden.

Muhammad was called to the prophetic mission when he was about forty years of age. Even before his prophethood, Muhammad(P.B.U.H) was an upright man, known for his integrity and truthfulness. He loved children. Having known early in life the pangs of being an orphan, he was always kind and concerned and generous to the orphans and the indigent. His being an orphan finds a place in the **Qurán**.

Did He not find you an orphan and shelter you?
Did He not find you wanting and guide you?
Did He not find you in need and provided for you?

**So do not oppress the orphan and do not repulse the beggar.
But rehearse and proclaim the bounty of your Lord. 93:6-11**

These verses also reflect the concern of Islam for the poor and the marginalized.

**And in your wealth is an acknowledged right
For the indigent and the outcast. 70:24**

All prophets including Abraham, Moses, and Jesus were vouchsafed supernatural powers by God in confirmation of their prophethood. These miracles were important tools as well in the propagation of the messages these prophets brought to their people. Muhammad is the only exception. His message relies solely on human nature, reason, and need for acceptance.

Qurán emphatically asserts that the message the prophet of Islam brought to his people is the same that was brought by various prophets to their people-from Noah to Abraham to Solomon, Jacob, Moses, and Jesus. The **Qurán** mentions twenty-five prophets.

The core message of all the prophets is the same: belief in the unity of God, belief in the Day of Judgment, doing righteous deeds such as fasting, taking care of the needy and the poor, and remembering God in their own way and shunning wrong doing.

The new strictly monotheistic message, belief in life after death and the Day of Judgment, preached by one of them had the potential to disrupt the economy of the Meccans. Muhammad was therefore up for serious opposition by his people who increasingly looked down upon him and shunned him. He was however protected by his powerful uncle who was the chief of Quraish. The uncle's death and the death of his wife in the same year, 619 CE, removed the umbrella of protection provided by them. His persecution by his own tribe increased many times and his life was in danger. He therefore, guided by divine inspiration, migrated to Medina-the city of his mother-another important city of the province of Hejaz, about 250 miles from Mecca. The prophet reached Quba, the southernmost part of the Medina oasis on September 4, 622 CE when he was about fifty-two years old. This date is also the beginning of the lunar based Muslim calendar known as the Hijra Era.

In Medina he was able to establish himself quickly as the first citizen of the city and rapidly became its acknowledged leader when he was able with his sagacity, compassion, impartiality, and political acumen, to unite and reconcile the many Arab factions antagonistic to each other. This brought peace to the warring city and enabled him to move rapidly towards the accomplishment of his mission according to his vision, which gradually evolved and developed, becoming more and more altruistic and universal in its scope. And what was his mission? To establish a polity where all faiths are recognized as aspects of truth:

Abraham the true in faith 4:125p

The Torah was revealed to Moses therein is guidance and light. 5:44p

We send Jesus the son of Mary, the gospel, therein is guidance and light. 5:46p

where greed and arrogance are treated as sins, where oppression in any form is not tolerated, even if it is from your own government or people, where human life, indeed all life, is sacred and not to be harmed without due process of law, where it is man's destiny to struggle on the high road of knowledge towards understanding of God and the universe of His creation and the Law governing His creation. That is the straight way, the way of God, the way of Law. Education, social justice, compassion, brotherhood, decent values, forgiveness, justice according to law, and respect towards all faiths and philosophies of life, equality of men and women in all respects are the important pillars of the polity he founded. Muhammad is the only prophet of God who has the distinction of founding a state in accordance with his mission, his vision. Before his death he was able to unite the many tribes of central Arabia into one single nation. He died in 632 CE and is buried in Medina, later named Medinatul-Nabi, which means "the city of the prophet." This city also has the distinction of being the first capital of the newly founded Islamic state.

By common consensus of the Ulema (Islamic scholars) the following verses marked the beginning of the momentous message revealed to the prophet of Islam.

Recite in the name of your Lord who created-
From an embryo created the human

Recite your lord is all-giving who taught by the pen
Taught the human what he did not know before. 96:1-5p
The following two verses also qualify for being the earliest revelations.
O you folded in garments stand by night, but not all night
Half of it or a little less or a little more.
And recite the Qurán in slow, measured, rhythmic tones.
Soon We shall send down to you a weighty message
Indeed, rising by night is most intense as a discipline
And most appropriate for receptivity to the Word. 73:1-6

O you wrapped up arise and warn and glorify your Lord
And keep your clothing clean and avoid filth;
And be generous without expecting any increase for yourself. 74:1-7
Important aspects of his message as listed in the **Qurán** are:

A Prophet for All Mankind

We have sent you only as a bearer of good news
And a warner for all mankind. 34:28

We have sent you the Book for mankind, according to truth. 39:41p

O people, the messenger has come to you with truth from your
Lord. 4:170p

Say, "O humanity I'm a messenger to you all from God,
To whom belongs the dominion of the heavens and the earth."
7:158p

It is a wonder for people that We inspired a man from among them
to warn humanity. 10:2p

A Book which We have revealed to you
That you may bring the people of the world out of darkness into
light. 14:1p

This is no less than a message to all the worlds
And you will certainly know the truth of it after a while. 38:87-88
We sent you not, but as a mercy to all creatures. 21:107

The Mission

We have sent to you a messenger from among you,
Who rehearses Our signs to you
And purifies you and instructs you in scripture and wisdom
And in new knowledge. 2:151

God did confer a great favor on the believers in sending into their midst
A messenger who is one of their own,
To rehearse God's signs to them and purify them
And instruct them in scripture and wisdom
Whereas they were in manifest error before. 3:164

Say, "What has come to me by inspiration is that your God is one God.
Will you therefore bow to His will?" 21:108

Say, "I am but a man like you. But inspiration has come to me
That your deity is one God-
So whoever hopes to meet his Lord, should act with integrity
And not compromise with anyone the worship of his Lord." 18:110

Say, "I am only a human like you, who has been inspired
That your deity is one God.
So be true to God and seek divine forgiveness.
And woe to the idolatrous those who don't give alms
And who scoff at the hereafter." 41:6-7

Say, "I am forbidden to worship those you invoke apart from God.
I will not follow your desire-if I do so, I shall be lost.
And not be one of those guided right."   6:56

People of scripture, Our messenger has come to you clarifying for you
After an intermission in the messengers
Lest you say "No bearer of good news has come to us and no warner"
So a bearer of good news and a warner has come to you.

And God is capable of all things 5:19

O prophet! Truly We have sent you as a witness,
A bearer of glad tidings, and a warner 33:45, 25:56

And as one who invites to God's
Grace by his leave; and as a lamp spreading light. 33:46

We have sent you only as a bearer of good tidings and warner
For all mankind. 34:28

You are only a warner. 35:23

We have sent you with truth to give glad tidings and to warn.
Never has there been a people to which a warner was not sent.   35:24
Also see **32:3, 38:65, 70, 46, 9, 48:8 27:92, 33:45-6**

We have sent by inspiration to you an Arabic Qurán so that you
may warn
The Mother of Cities (Makkah) and all around her;
And warn them of the day of Assembly of which there is no doubt;
Some will be in the garden and some in inferno. 42:7

So then give the call and be upright as you have been commanded.
Do not follow their vain desires and say, "I believe in whatever
Revelations God has bestowed from on high
And bidden to bring about equity in your mutual views."
God is our Sustainer and your Sustainer too.
We are responsible for our acts and you are responsible for your
acts.
Let there be no dispute between us.
God will unite us and the final goal is to God.   42:15

Say, "I am not the first of the messengers
And I do not know what will be done with me, or with you.
I follow only that which is revealed to me by inspiration.
I am but a warner open and clear."   46:9

We have sent you as a witness
And a harbinger of good news and a warner.   48:8

This is the word of a noble messenger, not the word of a poet,
Little do you believe. It is not the word of a diviner either.
Little do you reflect.
It is a revelation sent down from the Lord of the universe.
And if the messenger were to invent any saying in our name-
We should certainly seize him by his right hand
And we should certainly then cut off the artery of his heart.
Nor could any of you withhold him from our wrath. 69:40-47

Say, "I only pray to my Lord, with whom I associate no one." 72:20

Say, "It is not in my power to cause you any harm
Or to bring you to right conduct." 72:21

Say, "No one can grant me shelter from God if I were to disobey Him.
Nor could I find refuge except in God." 72:22

God (alone) knows the unseen.
He does not reveal the divine secrets to anyone,
Except His chosen messengers; then God sends scouts before and
after him,
So that they may know that he has
Delivered the messages of his Lord. 72:26-28p

O you folded in garments stand by night but not all night
Half of it or a little lessor a little more.
And recite the Qurán in slow measured and rhythmic tones.
We shall soon send you down a weighty word.
Truly the rising by night is a time when impression is keen
And most appropriate for receptivity to the word.
Truly during the day you have prolonged occupation with many
duties.
But remember the name of God,
And devote yourself whole heartedly to God. 73:1-8
O you folded in your mantle arise and warn.
Glorify your Lord and keep your garments clean and shun all
abominations.
Be generous without expecting much for yourself
And persevere in the way of your Lord. 74:1-7

So be constant to the command of your Lord,
And do not obey the sinner or the atheist among them. 76:24

Meditate upon the name of your Lord morning and evening.
And bow to God a part of the night and glorify God long into the
night. 76:25-26

By the glorious morning light, by the night when it is still:
Your Lord has not forsaken you nor is He displeased.
What is to come is better to you than what has gone before;
And soon your Lord will give you and you will be pleased.

93:1-6

He found you an orphan and gave shelter and care.
And God found you wandering, and guided you
He found you poor and enriched you-
Therefore, do not treat the orphan with harshness,
And do not repulse him who asks.
But rehearse and proclaim the bounty of your Lord. 93:6-11

Have We not expanded your breast?
And removed your burden which galled your back and exalted your
repute?
So with every distress there is relief. Verily with every distress there
is relief.
Therefore, when you are free, work diligently
And direct your attention to your Lord. 94:1-8

Recite in the name of your Lord who created from an embryo-
Created the human
Recite, "Your Lord is all giving: who taught by the pen-
Taught the human what he did not know before."
Oh, no! Man does indeed go to excess in looking upon himself as
self-sufficient.
Verily all return to you Lord. 96:1-8

A messenger from God reciting immaculate pages
In which are just decrees. 98:23

The Seal of Prophets

Muhammad is not the father of any of your men,
But the messenger of God, and the seal of the prophets. 33:40

This is the Same Message as Revealed to Noah and All Other Prophets

The same religion has He established for you which was enjoined on Noah,
By which We inspired you
And what We enjoined on Abraham, Moses, and Jesus. 42:13p

Say, "We believe in God and the revelation to us, and to Abraham, Ishmael,
Isaac, Jacob and the Tribes and that given to Moses and Jesus,
And that given to all prophets from their Lord.
We make no distinction between one and another of them
And we submit to God." 2:136

There is No Compulsion in Religion

There is no compulsion in religion; truth stands out clear from error.
So whoever repudiates idols and believes in God
Has taken hold of the most reliable handle which does not break. 2:256p

For We have sent you the Book for mankind, according to truth.
So whoever accepts guidance does so to the benefit of his own soul
And whoever strays only strays to the detriment of his own soul.
And you are not the one to dispose of their affairs. 39:41

You are not the disposer of their affairs. 42:6p

So if they turn away, we have not sent you as a guard over them:
Your only obligation is to convey. 42:48p

And to read the Qurán.
And whoever accepts guidance does so for the good of his own soul;
But if any one strays, then say, "I am only a warner." 27:92

Invite to the way of your Lord with wisdom and good advice,
And debate with others in the most dignified manner.
For your Lord knows best who is astray from the way of God
And knows best who are the ones who are guided. 16:125
Say, "O atheists I don't worship what you worship
And you don't worship what I worship
And I won't worship what you worship
And you won't worship what I worship.
To you your way and to me mine." 109:1-6

We know best what they say: but it is not for you to compel them by force.
So keep on reminding through the Qurán those who fear my warning. 50:45

And say to those who have been given scripture, and to the unlettered.
"Have you surrendered?"
And if they have surrendered then they are already guided
And if they turn away your only responsibility is to deliver the message. 3:20p

Whoever heeds the messenger is being obedient to God.
As for those who turn away,
We have not sent you to watch over them. 4:80

Insights from your Lord have already come to you:
So if any one sees, it is for his own benefit;
And if anyone is blind, it is to his own detriment.
Say, "I am not a guardian to watch over you." 6:104

Leave alone those who take their religion to be mere play and amusement
But proclaim the truth to them
That every soul delivers itself to perdition by its own acts. 6:70p
If they accuse you of false hood, say, "My work to me, and your work to you.
You are not responsible for what I do,
And I am not responsible for what you do." 10:41

Say, "Obey God, and obey the messenger of God,
But if you turn away, then his only obligation is his duty
And yours is your duty. If you obey him you will be guided.
But the messenger's only obligation is clear communication." 24:54

O prophet, say to the people of the Book,
"We believe in what is revealed to us and what was revealed to you
For our God and your God is one to Whom we submit." 29:46p

And say, "I believe in any scripture that God has revealed.
And I have been commanded to treat you all justly.
God is our Lord and your Lord too.
We are responsible for our acts, and you for your acts.
Let there be no argument between us.
God will unite us, and to Him is the final goal." 42:15p

In all this do you see force or compulsion playing a role in the propagation of Islam? The burden of the message is clear. If your mind accepts the message sent down to Muhammad (P.B.U.H) accept it; otherwise you go your way. But hold yourself responsible for the consequences of your choice.

Miracles

Unlike all other prophets mentioned in the **Qurán**, prophet Muhammad (P.B.U.H) was the only one who was not vouchsafed miracles to assist him in the propagation of his message, or as proof of his prophet hood.

They ask you about the end of time, when is it set,
Say, "Only the Lord has the knowledge of that." 7:187p

Say, "I have no power to profit or harm myself, except as God wills.
And if I know the un seen, I should have multiplied all good;
And no ill would have touched me.
I am just a warner, and a herald of good news to people who believe." 7:188

The unbelievers say, "Why is no miracle sent down to him by his Lord?"

Say, "You are only a warner and a guide to every nation." 13:7

They say, "Why were not signs from his Lord revealed to him?"
Say, "The signs are with God. I am only an open warner." 29:50

Say, "It is not in my power to cause you harm
Or to bring you to right conduct." 72:21

What you wish to see hastened is not in my power.
The command rests with God alone. 6:57p

Say, "What you would see hasten were in my power
The matter would be settled at once between you and me.
But God knows best those who are unjust." 6:58

With Him are keys of the unseen. 6:59

They swear their most powerful oaths by God,
That if a sign came to them they would surely believe in it.
Say the signs belong to God alone. 6:109p

Yet they say, "Why was a sign from his Lord not sent down to him?"
Say, "The unseen is up to God, so wait. Indeed I am waiting with
you." 10:20

And they say, "We will not believe you
Until you cause water to flow from earth for us as a fountain
Or you have a garden of dates and grapes, and
You cause streams to flow among them or you cause the sky to fall,
As you say will happen to us; or you bring God and the angels
before us
Or you have a house of gold. Or you ascend into the sky.
And we will not believe in your ascent
Until you should bring down a Book to read."
Say, "Glory to my Lord!
Am I anything but a human, a messenger?" 17:90-93

Muhammad is a human being like you, a messenger. 17:93p

Say, "I am only a human being like you." 18:110p

Say, "I am but a man like you." 42:6

Miscellaneous

When a (courteous) greeting is offered to you (Muhammad P.B.U.H)
Meet it with the greeting still more courteous or (at least)of equal courtesy
God takes careful account of all things 4:86

When you (Muhammad P.B.U.H) see them argue rashly about our signs
Withdraw from their company until they turn to a different theme.
In case the devil makes you forget
Leave the company of these unjust people the moment you remember. 6:68

Leave alone those who take their religion to be mere play and amusement
And are deceived by the life of this world. 6:70p

We only send you to give glad tidings and as a warner.
Say, "I do not ask any reward for it.
Other than that whoever will, may take a path to his Lord." 25:56-57

And do not follow the unbelievers and hypocrites, and ignore their insults;
And put your trust in God, for God is enough of a patron. 33:48

You are one of the messengers on a straight path.
So that you may warn a people whose ancestors had not been warned
And so they remain heedless. 36:6

Say, "I am not the first of the messengers
And I do not know what will be done with me. Or with you.
I only follow what has been revealed to me by inspiration.
And I am nothing but a plain warner." 46:9

Yes, I swear by the planets that recede, run and disappear;
And the night as it dissipates and the dawn as it breaks.

This is the word of a noble messenger endowed with power
His rank established in the presence of the Lord of the Throne
Obeyed and faithful there.
Your companion is not possessed.
Without doubt he saw Him in the clear horizon
And he is not grudging with the knowledge of the unseen
And this is not the word of a cursed devil
So where are you going? 81:15-26

Muhammad is only a messenger;
Other messengers have parted the way before him.
If he dies or is killed will you turn back on your heels?
If anyone turns back on his heels he will not
Harm God at all. 3:144p

Note In the last ten years of his mission when the Prophet had established a nascent Islamic state in Medina, his vision evolved and developed. The focus shifted onto mundane affairs. Islam seeks a balance between body and spirit, material and spiritual, and earthly and heavenly aspects of life. His endeavor was to establish a social dispensation as envisaged in the **Qurán**. This demanded governing by educated men of honor, wisdom, and compassion and guided by the sages amongst them. In the Islamic state education receives the highest priority, all faiths and their followers are respected, social justice and justice according to law prevail. Men and women are equal in all respects. Peace and safety are assured. Society is free from strife and oppression. Healing, compassion, and forgiveness are encouraged. All these and some aspects of relevance to today's world are the subject matter of this book.

The Qura'nic authority for what has been said in the note is found in different chapters. This has been excluded from here to avoid repetition.

Chapter Four

QURÁN AND KNOWLEDGE (ILM)

Qurán is not for the illiterates. 2:78p
God has revealed the Book to you.
In it are verses basic or fundamental.
They are the matrix of the Book and others are not so clear.
No one knows its explanation but God and those deeply rooted
in knowledge. 3:7p

O, society of sprites and humans,
if you can penetrate the ranges of the heavens and the earth,
then go ahead.
But you cannot penetrate without acquiring the Law.   55:33

Chapter 4

Qurán and Knowledge

Acquiring knowledge (ILM) is the most important pillar of Islamic polity. Nearly one tenth of the **Qurán** underlines the vital importance of knowledge and learning. **Qurán** means reading. Let us look at the very first verses revealed to Muhammad (P.B.U.H)

Read in the name of your Lord
Who created from an embryo-created the human.
Read your Lord is all giving who taught by the pen.
Taught the human what he did not know before. 96:1-5

"Read" is the first word of the momentous opening revelation. Read, know, taught, and pen figure six times in these five verses. And creation, God's preeminent activity is an important outcome of knowledge. Creation of the human from an embryo? Embryology is an appropriate branch of modern scientific knowledge to merit mention in the very first revelation. Is it any wonder then that **Qurán** assigns the highest priority to learning?

Knowledge and the faculty to acquire knowledge are what distinguish humans from angels. Angels are the symbol of good. They only obey and have been given limited knowledge. Man, on the contrary, has unlimited capacity to learn. And has access to all branches of knowledge. Man has also been blessed with the freedom of choice-the ability to choose from more than one option available to him in a given situation. Angels have been denied the option to choose. It is for this reason that God commands angels to bow to Adam, the repository of vast knowledge and the archetypal human.

When your Lord said to the angels, "I will place a vice-jerent on earth"
They submitted, "Will you place on earth
One who will make mischief there and shed blood?
Whereas we celebrate your praises and glorify Your holy name?"
God said, "I know what you do not know."
And He taught Adam names (nature, reality, and causes)of all things.
God then placed them before the angels and said:
"Tell Me the names of these, if you are right.
They said glory to you! Of knowledge we have none except what you taught us
In truth it is You who are perfect in knowledge and wisdom."
He said "O Adam. Tell them their names."
When he told them their names, God said, "Did I not tell you that I know
The secrets of heavens and earth?
And I know what you reveal and what you conceal."
We said to the angels "Bow down to Adam" and they bowed down,
Not so iblis (Mephistopheles),
He refused and was haughty, he was the scoffer. 2:30-34

Thus an angel who refused to bow to Adam, the symbol of the supremacy of knowledge, fell, and the fallen angel became an embodiment of evil. It is therefore reasonable to conclude that ignorance is evil and leads to superstition. If humankind wants to get rid of evil from society, it should shed ignorance and illiteracy, and acquire more and more knowledge. Knowledge of what? Of sciences, history, archaeology, philosophy, metaphysics, knowledge of the world around man, of man himself, of life, of Light, of the ultimate Reality, of the Truth, his environment, atmosphere, and the cosmic world and the law governing the universe. This will be evident as we progress in this chapter.

We have sent among you a messenger of your own.
Rehearsing to you Our signs and purifying you
And instructing you in scripture and wisdom. And in new knowledge. 2:151
This book is not for the illiterates, they know not the Book,
And seek their own desires and indulge in conjecture. 2:78

God has revealed the Book to you, in it are verses basic or fundamental.

They are the matrix of the Book, and others are not so clear
No one knows its explanation, but God, and those deeply rooted
in knowledge.
And none will grasp the message except men of understanding. 3:7

And it is so that those to whom knowledge has been given
May know that it is the truth from Your Lord,
So they may believe in God and their hearts may be humbled
to God.
For God is the guide of those who believe, to a straight path. 22:54

But those among them who are well-grounded in knowledge,
We shall soon give a great reward. 4:162p

We have propounded for people in this Qurán every kind of parable.
The parables We set for mankind
Only those understand them who have knowledge. 29:43 and 30:58

The **Qurán** does not believe in form without content, belief without knowledge. In one sense, belief is concerned only with the appearances of things. It is a function of knowledge to permeate to the underlying reality.

We may remind ourselves that the highway of knowledge is straight and infinite. We will have to wait until mankind has learned all there is to know before it claims to have known the Reality, the Truth, the God. Man's civilized life is less than ten-thousand years old. Measured with the cosmic scale, this is less than the time it takes to blink. Man has just started walking on the highway of knowledge, and the end is trillions miles away.

Meanwhile, during man's long, long, journey on the path leading to God, he may have changed and evolved into a form altogether different and unrecognizable to today's man-**the final genesis** as the **Qurán** says:

We are not to be frustrated from changing your forms
In creating you in forms that you know not.
Your already know the first creation, so why not take a lesson?
56:60p, 61-2

The **Qurán's** primary audience is the educated and the wise, those who are engaged in understanding the signs of God, the parables, oaths etc. And to those who are dedicated to understanding the reality behind appearances, the daily phenomenon, the nature around us, the cosmos and the laws governing it. In short, they are the people who are engaged in discovering the causes of things. They are the intellectual giants of the time, the inspired ones, the Noble laureates, men of letters, the philosophers, the historians, the economists, the wise, the men of faith, of understanding, the thoughtful, those who contemplate, and most of all, the scientists.

The **Qurán** is a book of signs. Signs, oaths, parables, and similitudes are the mediums God frequently uses to communicate with humans.

And God shows you His signs
Now which of the signs of God do you deny? 40:81

Indeed, in the creation of the heavens and the earth,
And the alteration of the night and the day,
And the ships that sail the seas for the benefit of humanity,
And the water God sends down from the sky,
With which God enlivens the earth after its death,
And distributes all kinds of animals thereupon,
And the coursing of the winds and the clouds employed between sky and earth
Surely there are signs for people who are wise. 2:164
Those who remember God standing, sitting, and lying on their sides
Contemplating the creation of the heavens and the earth
With the saying of our Lord, You did not create this in vain. 3:191p

It is God who causes the grain and the date-stone to split and sprout
God brings forth the living from the dead
And is the One who brings forth the dead from the living
That is God for you. Then how are you deluded away from the truth? 6:95

And it is God who causes water to descend from the sky
And reproduce thereby sprouts of every thing from which we produce greenery,
From which we produce heaps of grain;
And from the date palm clusters of fruit hanging from its spathes;

And groves of grapes, and olive sand pomegranates, similar but
unlike,
Behold their fruit when they bear and in its ripeness
Surely in that are signs for people who believe. 6:99

And God is the one who created you all from one soul,
A residence and a repository.
We have made the signs clear to people who understand. 6:98

Are they equal those who know and those who do not know?
Only those endowed with reason take heed. 39:9p

By the dawn, by the night's ten, by the odd and the even
By the night as it eases away
Is there not in that an oath for the thoughtful? 89:1-5

And God is the One who made the stars for you
That you may be guided by them in the darkness by land and sea
We have made the signs to people who are discerning. 6:97

O society of sprites and humans,
If you can penetrate the ranges of the heavens and the earth
Then go ahead. But you cannot penetrate without acquiring the
law. 55:33

It is God who made the sun radiant and the moon glow
And appointed its stations that you may know
To compute years and the calculation
God did not create them but with deliberation
God distinctly explains His signs for those who know. 10:5

Another of His signs is the lightning He shows
To fill you with fright and hope. 30:24p

God has subjected the night to you and the day, and the sun and
the moon,
And the stars are subject, by the Divine order.
Surely in these are signs for people who are wise. 16:12

And your Lord inspired the bee to make their hives,

In the mountains, in the trees, and habitations
Then eat from all the fruits, gently walking the pathways of your
Lord
From within them exudes a drink of various colors,
In it is healing for mankind.
Surely in that is a sign for people who reflect. 16:68-69

And we created pairs of everything that you may contemplate. 51:19

Do not the unbelievers see that the heavens and the earth
Were one integrated mass, then we split them.
And made every living thing from water. Now won't they believe?
21:30

Do they not travel the earth and see what was the end of those
before them?
They were more numerous than these and superior in strength
And in their effects on the earth.
But what they had achieved did not profit them. 40:82 and 35:44p

The One who created seven skies in correspondence,
You see no disharmony in the creation of the Benevolent One.
Now look. Do you see any gap? Then look twice again.
And your vision will come back to you weak and weary. 67:3-4

Have they not seen the birds above them
As they draw in their wing shaving spread them
The Benevolent One alone holds them up, observing everything.
67:19
And in your constitution and scattering of animals through the
earth
Are signs for those who are sure. 45:4

God has subjected the sea to you,
And He subjected to you what is in the heavens and what is on
earth.
Surely there are signs in that for those who reflect 45:12p, 13

Those to whom knowledge has been given

May know that this Qurán is the truth from their Lord. 22:54p

Those to whom knowledge has been given realize that
What has been revealed by their Lord is the truth
And leads to the path of God. 34:6p

Travel the earth and see how those who repudiated the truth ended
up. 6:11

Travel the earth and see how God originated the creation
And God will produce the final genesis. 29:20
Do they not see how God initiates the creation, then renews it?
20:19p

For God has sent down to you the book and wisdom
And taught you what you knew not.
And great is the grace of God to you. 4:113

Those among you who are well-grounded in knowledge
And the believers, believe in what has been revealed to you
And what was revealed before you and believe in God and in the
last day
And those who establish regular prayer and pay the zakat;
To them shall We soon give a great reward. 4:162

And the keys of the unseen are with God who alone knows them
And God knows what is on the land and in the sea.
Not a leaf falls but God knows it and there is not a single grain
In the darknesses of earth, and nothing green and nothing dry,
But is inscribed in the record clear to those who can read.6:59

Now such were their houses in utter ruin-because they practiced
wrongdoings;
Verily in this is a sign for people of knowledge. 27:52

And among His signs are the variations in your languages and your
colors
And these are signs for those who know. 30:22

Glory to God who created in pairs all things,

All of them from what the earth produces
As well as their own selves and things of which they have no
knowledge. 36:36

By the sun and his splendor, by the moon as she follows him
By the day as it shows up the sun's glory, by the night as it conceals it
By the firmament and its wonderful structure, by the earth and its
expanse
By the soul, and the proportion and order given to it
And its inspiration as to its wrong and its right
Truly he succeeds that purifies it and he fails that corrupts it.
91:1-10

No change will you find in the law of God 33:62p

Even such words as heaven, day, night, hell, the day of reckoning,
and angels are "sign" words and await to be fully understood and
explained by men of knowledge. At one place God swears by time.

By the time, man is indeed at a loss. 103:12

What is time? Read Stephen Hawkins' book on time to understand
what it is that God is swearing by. If an airplane is hurtling through
space, time slows down, and if it attains the seed of light, time stops.
One of the most potent prayers in the **Qurán** is:

O My Lord! Increase me in knowledge. 20:114p

Thus for full understanding of God and the **Qurán**, the highly
educated persons are God's chosen instrument. It is their responsibility to
discover the Law of God, make it known to mankind, so that everyone
lives in accordance with the Law. If this species does not play the game,
the Creator will not hesitate to blot it out and replace it with other species
in forms which today's man may not be able to recognize, (refer 56:60p,
61-2, already quoted on page 94) who nonetheless will observe the Law.
For mankind at large, the **Qurán** demands social justice, justice
according to law, full opportunities for education, equality of men and
women in all respects, respect for all faiths, and tolerance and regard
for human rights and comfortable living with peace.

Chapter Five

ISLAM AND OTHER RELIGIONS

The same religion He has established for you
As that which He enjoined on Noah
That which We have sent by inspiration to you
And that which we enjoined on Abraham, Moses, and Jesus.
42:13p

The Muslims, the Jews, the Christians and the Sabians
Who believe in God and the last day and are righteous
Have their reward with their Lord.
There is nothing for them to fear; nor shall they sorrow.   2:62
To each among you We have established a law and a revealed
way.   5:48p
O Prophet, say to the people of the Book,
"We believe in what is revealed to us and what was revealed
to you
For our God and your God is one to Whom we submit." 29:46

Chapter 5

Islam and Other Religions

The **Qurán** asserts again and again that the revelation vouchsafed to Prophet Muhammad (P.B.U.H) is in the tradition of the revelations given to all prophets ((the **Qurán** mentions twenty-five of them) including Noah, Abraham, David, Solomon, Jacob, Moses, and Jesus.

The same religion He has established for you
As that which He enjoined on Noah
That which We have sent by inspiration to you
And that which we enjoined on Abraham, Moses, and Jesus. 42:13p

Nothing is said to you that was not said to the messengers before you. 41:43p

Significantly, the following chapters of the **Qurán** are named after some prophets and Mary, the mother of Jesus.

1. Chapter 10 is named after Jonah (Yunus) (P.B.U.H)
2. Chapter 11 is named after Hud (P.B.U.H)
3. Chapter 12 is named after Joseph (P.B.U.H)
4. Chapter 14 is named after Abraham (P.B.U.H) His name occurs in more than 125 verses
5. Chapter 19 is named after Mary, mother of Jesus The **Qurán** subscribes to her immaculate conception and mentions her name in 55 verses
6. Chapter 71 is named after Noah (P.B.U.H)

7. Chapters 47, (by name) and 73 and 74 (by his titles) are named after Muhammad (P.B.U.H)

Recognizing and honoring all the prophets is an essential article of a Muslim's faith. Islam thus recognizes the validity of all earlier prophets, their revelations, and the books.

The messenger believes in what has been revealed to him from his Lord
As do the men of faith.
Each one of them believes in God, His angels, His Books and His messengers.
We make no distinction between one and another of His messengers
And they say we hear and we obey-We ask your forgiveness, our Lord,
For our destiny leads to You. 2:285p

O Prophet, say to the people of the Book,
"We believe in what is revealed to us and what was revealed to you
For our God and your God is one to Whom we submit." 29:46

And say, "I believe in any scripture that God has revealed.
And I have been commanded to treat you all justly.
God is our Lord and your Lord too.
We are responsible for our acts, and you for your acts.
Let there be no argument between us.
God will unite us, and to Him is the final goal." 42:15p

And they say, "We believe in God and the revelation given to us,
And to Abraham, Ismael, Isaac, Jacob, and the Tribes
And that given to Moses and Jesus and that given to all prophets,
From their Lord. We make no difference between one and the other of them
And we submit to God'." 21:36

We have inspired you as we inspired Noah and messengers after him:
We inspired Abraham, Ishmael, Isaac, Jacob, and the Tribes,
To Jesus, Job, Jonah, Aaron, and Solomon,
And to David we gave the psalms. 4:163

And Zacharias and John and Jesus and Elias. All in the rank of righteous. 6:85

To them and to their fathers and progeny and brethren
We chose them and we guided them to the straight way
This is the guidance of God. If they were to join other gods with Him
All that they did would be vain for them
These were the men to whom we gave the Book
And the judgment and prophet hood
If their descendants reject them behold we shall entrust their charge
To a new people who will not reject them. 68:85-89

This is a Book We have revealed, blessed, verifying what preceded. 6:92

The Muslims, the Jews, the Sabians,
The Christians, the Magians*, and the polytheists

God will judge between them on the Day of Judgment. 22:17
By the fig and the olive and the Mount Sinai and this city of security. 95:123

Mount Sinai refers to Judaism, and the city of security to Mecca, and hence to Islam. Olive refers to the Mount of Olives just outside Jerusalem and points to Christianity and to other faiths of the region such as the Sabians.

Fig points to the faiths of northern India where it grows wildly, as well as cultivated extensively, like olive in the Palestinian region. Fig therefore refers to the ancient Vedic religions. It has also been authoritatively suggested that the fig stands for the Ficus Indica, the Bo-tree under which Gautama Buddah received enlightenment. Thus the Bo-tree is sacred to the Vedic religions as well as to Buddism. (reference A. Yusuf Ali translation of the HOLY QURA'N-Note 6198 to Surah 95)

Now what is the core message that these messengers brought to their people?

The Muslims, the Jews, the Christians and the Sabians

---

* The Magians are the followers of the Iranian propher Zoroaster, who is said to have lived and preached about six -hundred years BCE. Their scripture is Zend-Avesta

Who believe in God and the last day and are righteous
Have their reward with their Lord.
There is nothing for them to fear; nor shall they sorrow. 2:62
Those to whom scripture was given were commanded only
  a. To worship God sincerely in their way of life
  b. To believe in the Day of Judgment
  c. To practice regular prayers
  d. And give zakat (financial assistance)

To the poor, to the orphan, the widow, the needy wayfarer,

And to free a slave
This is true religion 98:4p-5

As for those who disbelieved
Both among the peoples of scripture and polytheists,
They will be in hell fire. They are the worst of creation. 98:6p

Those who have faith and do righteous deeds
They are the best of creation
Their reward is in the presence of their Lord:
Gardens of eternity where they will abide forever. 98:7,8p

This undoubtedly includes the Jews, the Christians, the Hindus,
the Zoroastrians, and followers of other religions.

Among the people of the scripture is a community that is upright,
Read the signs of God through the night prostrating themselves.
They believe in God and the last day; and they enjoin what is fair
And forbid what is repugnant. And hasten to good deeds.
They are the righteous. And whatever good they do will not be
denied them;
God knows the conscientious. 3:113p, 114-115

Believers believe in God and God's messengers,
And the scripture that God has sent down to his messenger
And the scripture which He sent down before.
Any who denied God, His Angels, His Books,

His messengers and the Day of Judgment has gone far, far astray.
4:136

To each among you We have established a law and a revealed way.
5:48p

We have sent our messengers with clear signs and We sent them
the Book
And the balance so that humanity may stand by justice. 57:25p

This is true of all faiths. Bypassing other faiths, I will discuss in some detail only Judaism and Christianity. And a verse on Abraham before that.

And who is better in faith than the one who surrenders his being
to God,
And is a doer of good, and follows the way of Abraham, rightly
guided!
For God took Abraham as a friend. 4:125

Judaism

Moses is the prophet most mentioned in the **Qurán**. There are nearly four hundred verses on him and his people. I'm only quoting the verses relating to the core of the message.

God said, "Moses, I have chosen you
Over the people by My mission and by My word,
So take what I have given you and be among the grateful." 7:144
And We wrote of all things for him on the Tablets, counsel and
judgment on all things. 7:144p

When Moses came to Our appointment and his Lord spoke to him,
He said, "My Lord appear before me that I may look at You"
God said, "You will never see Me but look at the mountain-
If it remains in its place then you will see Me."
But when the Lord manifested to the mountain in his effulgence
It crumbled to a heap of dust and Moses fell down thunderstruck.
When he recovered he said, "Glory to You. I turn to you repentant

And am the first of the believers." 7:143

And we gave Moses the Book and the criterion. 2:53p

Now has the story of Moses reached you?
When he saw a fire he said to his family, 'Wait, for I perceive a fire;
Perhaps I can bring you a live coal from it, or find direction at the fire"
Then when he reached it, he was called
"O Moses! I am your Lord. So remove your sandals,
For you are in the holy valley Tuwa and I have chosen you
So listen to what is revealed I am the God, there is no deity but Me
So serve Me and practice prayer to remember Me
For the end of time is coming, but I plan to conceal it,
So that every soul is rewarded for its effort
So do not let anyone who disbelieves in it
And follows his own desires, alienate you from it,
For you would be destroyed." 20:9-16

We did send Moses with Our signs and clear authority. 40:23

We give Moses the guidance and bequeath scripture to the offspring
Of Israel as guidance and reminder for those endowed with reason.
40:53-54

O children of Israel! Remember my blessing with which I have blessed you
And I fulfill my promise; fulfill your promise. And let it be Me that you fear
And believe in what I have revealed to you
And do not sell my signs for a petty price; and be mindful of Me
And do not cover truth with falsehood and do not conceal truth knowingly
And pray regularly, and give alms
And bow down with those who bow. 2:40, 41p, 42-43
Those who believe they are to meet their Lord
That is where their destiny leads. 2:46

O children of Israel! Remember my blessing, with which I have blessed you;
And that I have favored you above all nations
And beware of a day when no soul can compensate for another soul
For anything, and no intercession will be accepted from one,
And no ransom will be taken from one and they will not be helped.
2:48

The **Qurán** mentions Moses' many miracles such as:

1. gushing forth twelve springs of water for his twelve tribes when Moses struck a rock with his staff
2. the parting of the sea to make way for Moses and his people to escape to safety and drowning of pharaoh and his army in full view of Moses
3. supply of manna and quails
4. Moses's upbringing from infancy in the palace of the pharaoh
5. his return to Egypt with Aaron on his side and with the magical staff in his hand to confront the pharaoh, etc.

<u>Jesus</u>

And the angels said,
"O Mary, God has chosen you over the women of all peoples,
And purified you." 3:42

Mary, obey your Lord devoutly, worship and go down in prayer
With those who bow down in prayer. 3:43

The angel said, "O Mary, God gives you good news of a Word from God
Named the Messiah, Jesus, son of Mary,
Honored in the world and the hereafter and one of the intimates of God.
And he will speak to the people in infancy and maturity,
And be one of the righteous." 3:45-46

And God will teach him scripture
And wisdom and the Torah and the Gospel. 3:48

Jesus said, "It is God that is my Lord and your Lord,
So serve God; that is a straight path." 3:51

And we gave Jesus the Gospel, with guidance and truth in it
And guidance and counsel for the conscientious. 5:46p

Jesus said, "I am indeed the servant of God,
Who has given me the scripture and made me a prophet
And made me blessed wherever I am;
And has prescribed prayers and charity for me as long as I live."
19:30-31

We sent Jesus, son of Mary with the Gospel;
And we put kindness and mercy in the heart of those who follow
him. 57:27p

We gave Jesus, son of Mary, clear proofs
And strengthened him with the holy spirit. 2:87p

The Jews claimed we killed the Messiah,
Jesus, Son of Mary, messenger of God
Whereas they did not kill him, and they did not crucify him
Although it was made to seem thus to them
Rather God raised him up to the divine presence. 4:158p

Those who say messiah, son of Mary is God, have blasphemed. 5:17p

And peace is upon me the day I was born and the day I die
And the day I am resurrected alive
That was Jesus, son of Mary a word of truth about which they
doubt. 19:33-34

Qurán mentions many miracles vouchsafed to Jesus Christ such as
his speaking in infancy, his raising the dead, his healing the leper and
the blind etc.

The similarity among the three faiths, namely, Islam, Judaism, and
Christianity as revealed to their prophets, is truly stunning and needs
to be brought onto the center stage of interfaith forums.

To each among you we have established a law and a revealed way. 5:48p

This chapter needs be read along with chapters 2 and 3 to clearly and fully understand Islam's stand on other religions. Some important verses have been taken out to avoid repetition.

Chapter Six

SOCIAL JUSTICE

Righteousness is not that you should turn
Your faces to the East or West;
The righteous are those who spend of their substance on the
indigent.   2:177p

They ask you how much they are to spend in charity.
Say: whatever is beyond your needs.   2:219p

The believers are those who pray and give alms and are sure
of the hereafter.   27:1-3p

In your wealth there is an acknowledged right for the poor and
the marginalized.   70:24, 25

Chapter 6

Social Justice

Social justice is one of the most important pillars of Islamic polity and social dispensation. God equates charity with faith. Giving is next in importance to belief in one God, the Day of Judgment, and acquiring knowledge. Those who are seeking the countenance of God and wish to be prosperous must give what is due to the poor. Safeguard yourselves from avarice if you want to thrive. Those who give of their wealth become pure. Those who do not share their wealth with the deserving are idolaters. God is a friend of those who spend in charity, in good times and in bad. The charitable persons are truly righteous.

Islam detests poverty. It is a religion of shared prosperity. It is obligatory on the well to do and the government to take care of the poor, the widow, the orphan, the needy, and the wayfarer, of those who ask and those who do not ask out of shame, the vulnerable and the marginalized, without discrimination of color, creed, or nationality. It is also incumbent on a Muslim to help the neighbor in straitened circumstances.

Charity expiates some of your evil. Do not be stingy. Do not be extravagant, lest you become reprehensible and destitute.

Zakat is an obligatory financial levy on the enabled members of the Muslim Ummah (the entire community.) Zakat literally means purification of one's wealth and spiritual purification. How much is one to set aside as zakat?

What is beyond your needs? 2:219p

On the Day of Judgment, a person who is given the record in the left hand is the one who did not believe in Almighty God and did not encourage feeding the poor. The reward of the Day of Judgment is reserved for those who believe in God and who share their wealth with the indigent, who do not squander away their wealth in vanities. Do they think that their wealth will last forever? Those who in charity spend by night and by day, in secret and in public, have their reward with their Lord. They will not grieve. And the nation that neglects the poor will be substituted by another who will be generous to the poor and the marginalized. There is a recognized right in your wealth for the poor. Whatever you spend in the way of God strengthens your soul and is a loan to God that will be paid back a thousand fold.

There are three more dimensions to charity. Firstly, do not nullify your charity by reminders of your generosity. Be graceful in giving. Do not hurt the dignity and self-respect of the recipient. Secondly, in giving choose the good things-not the bad ones, something which you yourself would not take. Thirdly, if you have given a loan to someone and if he is in difficulty in repayment, give him time until it is easy for him to repay. But if you remit it altogether, it is best for you.

The following verses of the **Qurán** bear out what has been said.

Righteousness is not that you should turn
Your faces to the East and to the West;
The righteous are those who believe in God and the last day
And the angels and the Book and the Messengers;
To spend of your substance out of love for Him, for your relatives,
The orphans, the poor, and the traveler.
For those who ask and to free the slaves and who pray regularly
and give zakat
And who fulfill their promises when they promise,
To be firm and patient in misfortune, affliction and hard times.
Such are the people of the truth, the God fearing. 2:177

And pray regularly and give zakat;
And whatever good you send for your souls, you will find with
God. 2:110p

And spend of your substance for the sake of God,
And do not let your own hands contribute to (your) ruin but do good,
For God loves those who do good. 2:195

They ask you what they should spend.
Say, "Whatever you spend that is good; is for parents and relatives
And orphans and those in want and for the traveler."
And whatever good you do God knows all about it. 2:215

They ask you how much they are to spend (in charity).
Say, "Whatever is beyond your needs."
Thus God clarifies the signs to you so that you may reflect. 2:219p

The parable of those who spend their wealth in the way of God
Is that of a grain of corn: it grows seven ears, and each ear has a
hundred grains.
And God may choose to multiply anyone at will.
And God cares for all and He is all-knowing
Those who spend their wealth in the cause of God and do not
follow up
Their gifts with reminders of their generosity or with injury
Have their reward with their Lord; they will not suffer fear,
Nor will they grieve. 2:261-2

Kind and forgiving words are better than charity followed by injury.
God is free of all wants. 2:263p

O believers! Do not nullify your charities by reminder of your generosity
Like those who spend their money to be seen of men.
They are like hard barren rock with some dust on it.
Hit by heavy rain leaves it barren.
They can do nothing with what they have earned.
For God does not guide atheistic people,
Those who spend their money seeking to please God
And to strengthen their own souls are like a garden on a hill;
When heavy rain hits, it brings forth double its fruits.
And if heavy rain does not fall then dew is sufficient.
For God sees what you do. 2:264-5

O believers, give of the good things you have earned,
And from what We have produced for you from the earth.
And do not choose the bad there-from to give away something
Which you would not take it except with closed eye.

And know that God is free of all wants and worthy of praise
Satan threatens you with poverty and compels you to indecencies,
Whereas God promises you divine forgiveness and bounties
And God is all-embracing, all knowing. 2:267-8

And whatever you spend in charity surely God knows it. 2:270p

If you disclose acts of charity that's fine, but if you conceal them
And get them to the needy quietly, that is better for you.
It will expiate some of your evils. And God is aware of what you
do. 2:271

Those who give of their wealth, night and day, secretly and openly,
Have their reward with their Lord;
No fear will be on them, and they will not grieve. 2:274
Those who spend in good times and bad,
And those who restrain anger and those who forgive people
God loves those who do good. 3:134

Your only friends are God, His messengers and the believers,
Those who pray regularly and give zakat and bow down. 5:55

My mercy extends to those who do right and pay zakat
And those who believe in our signs. 7:156p

Those who slander and ridicule the believers who
Willingly give charitable donations
As well as those who give according to their means,
God will ridicule them; and there is a painful punishment for them.
9:79

Worship God, and do not associate anything with God.
Be good to your parents and relatives and orphans and paupers
And close neighbors and distant neighbors and the companion by
your side,
And travelers on the road, and those in your legitimate custody
For God does not love anyone who is arrogant and vain. 4:36

Those who are stingy and get people to be stingy,
Hiding what God has given them from the divine bounty

We have prepared a humiliating penalty for the atheists. 4:37

And give relatives their due and the poor and the wayfarer,
But do not squander wastefully; for squanderers are brothers of
the devil;
And the devil is ungrateful to his Lord. 17:26,27P

And do not keep your hand bound to your neck
Nor yet stretch it as for as it extends,
Lest you become reprehensible and destitute. 17:29

The believers are sure to succeed: those who are humble in their
prayers,
And those who avoid vain talk and those who are active in charity.
23:1-4
These are verses of the Qurán, a clarifying Book,
Guidance and good news for the believers
Those who pray regularly and give alms
And who are sure of the hereafter. 27:1-3

So give what is due to the kindred, the needy, and the wayfarer,
That is best for those who seek the Countenance, of God,
And it is they who will prosper.
That which you give in usury for increase through the property
Of (other) people will have no increase with God;
But that which you give for charity, seeking the countenance of God,
It is these who will get a recompense multiplied. 30:38-9

These are Verses of the wise book a Guide and a Mercy to the Doers
of Good.
Those who establish regular Prayer, and give zakat and have sure
faith in the hereafter.
These are on (true) guidance from their Lord:
And these are the ones who will prosper. 30:2-5

And woe to those who join gods with God,-
Those who pay not zakat and who even deny the Hereafter. 41:6p

Behold, you are those invited to spend in the Way of God:

But among you are some that are niggardly, but any who are niggardly
Are so at the expense of their own souls.
God is free of all wants, and it is you that are needy.
If you turn back (from the path) He will substitute in your stead
another people who would not be like you. 47:38

Believe in God and the Messenger of God,
And spend in charity of what we have made you inheritors to.
For those of you who do have faith and expend
There is a great reward for them. 57:7

Believers! When you consult the Messenger in private,
Spend something in charity before your private consultation.
That is best for you, But if you do not have the means,
God is very forgiving, most merciful. 58:12p
Whatever God has awarded to the messenger of God
From the people of the cities, is for God, and the messenger of God,
And for relative and orphans, and the destitute, and travelers,
So that it won't circulate among the wealthy in your midst. 59:7p

And give of what We have provided you,
Before death comes to one of you and he says,
"My Lord, why did not You let me stay awhile-
I would have given in charity, and would be among the righteous."
But God will not let a soul stay behind when its time has come
And God is fully aware of what you do. 63:10-11

So be conscious of God, as much as you can,
And listen and obey and contribute for your own good
And those who safeguard themselves from avarice
They are the ones who thrive. If you advance God a good loan,
God will multiply it for you, and forgive you;
For God is most appreciative, most clement. 64:17-17

For those who accumulate a hoard,
For man was created anxious,
unhappy when ill afflicts him and stingy when good befalls him
Their fate is a raging fire.

and those in whose wealth is an acknowledged right
for the beggar and the outcast,
they will be honored in gardens. 70:18-21, 24-25,35

Read as much of the Qurán as it is easy, and pray regularly and
give alms,
Lending a good loan to God, or whatever good you advance
For the sake of your souls,
You will find it in God better and greater in reward. 73:20p

And ask of the sinners: "What led you into hell fire?
We were not of those who fed the indigent:
But we used to talk vanities with vain talkers:
And we used to deny the Day of Judgment
Until there came to us (the hour) that is certain." 74:41-42, 44

As for the righteous, they feed for the love of God,
The poor, the orphan, and the captive.
We are feeding you solely for the sake of God:
We want no compensation from you, not even thanks. 7:65p,68-69

And as for man, whenever his Lord tests him
By honoring him and pampering him
He says, "My Lord has honored me!"
And when his Lord tests him by restricting his provision,
He says, "My Lord has insulted me!"
It's not that, but you are not generous to the orphan
And do not encourage each other to feed the poor
And you consume inheritance with all-consuming voracity
And you love wealth with inordinate love. 89:15-20

And We showed him the two highways but he has not braved the
steep road
And what will convey to you what the steep road is?
Emancipation of a slave or feeding on a day of hunger
An orphaned relative or a destitute pauper. 90:10-16

As for those who are
Generous and conscientious, trusting in the happy end

We will facilitate ease for them
And for those who are stingy and complacent
Repudiating the happy end we will facilitate hardship for them
And their wealth won't help them when they fall. 92:4-11

But the most conscientious will be kept away from it (the raging fire)
Those who give of their wealth to become pure
Without any favor to be repaid to anyone
Only seeking the acceptance of their supreme Lord;
And they will be satisfied. 92:17-21

Did God not find you orphaned and give shelter?
And God found you wandering and gave guidance
And God found you needy and gave sufficiency
So don't oppress the orphan and don't rebuff the seeker
And rehearse and proclaim the bounty of your Lord. 93:6-11

Do you see the one who rejects religion?
That is the one who rebuffs the orphan
And does not encourage feeding the poor.
So woe to those who pray yet are inattentive to their prayer,
Those who want to be seen but refuse to supply even neighborly
needs. 107:1-7

Do you recognize the superiority of establishing social justice in a
Muslim polity?

Chapter Seven

WOMEN IN MUSLIM POLITY

To men is allotted what they earn.
And to women what they earn.   *4:32p*

If you fear that you cannot do justice by the orphans,
Marry women of your choice two, or three, or four,
But if you fear that you shall not be able to deal with them
equitably,
Then marry only one.   *4:3p*

You are never able to do justice between wives,
Even if it is your ardent desire.   *4:129p*

If a woman fears abuse or desertion from her husband, there
is no blame if they make a peaceful settlement, for peace is
best. 4:128p

Chapter 7

Women in Muslim Polity

Like Jihad, the status of women in Islam has been much maligned and much misunderstood by the West and most of all, by the Muslim scholars themselves. Christianity has to some extent influenced the attitude of the Muslim scholars. Unlike Islam, Christianity does not permit women to speak in the church, or teach, or baptize. They are not allowed to claim for themselves a share in masculine functions. Women cannot hold priestly offices. They should quietly receive instructions in complete obedience and not act superior to man. **Women should adorn themselves in well-arranged dresses with modesty, not with style of hair braided and gold or pearl or very expensive garb. The first to Timothy, Chapter 1, Acts of Apostles**

Your wives be in subjection to your husbands. Colossians 3:18

Christianity holds Eve, not Adam, responsible for the fall of man. One Timothy

Islam, on the contrary, holds Adam, not Eve responsible for the fall of man.

**And We said, "Adam, dwell in the garden,
Do not approach this particular tree, lest you become wrongdoers."
2:35p**

But Satan whispered evil to him. 20:120p

**In the result, they both ate of the tree,
Thus Adam disobeyed His Lord, and fell into error. 20:121p**

Thus Adam, the archetypal man exercising his newly acquired gift to choose from different options, makes the wrong choice and falls.

Chapter 4 of the **Qurán** is named "The Women." No chapter is named to honor the male gender.

Chapter 19 is named after Mary, the Mother of Jesus. No chapter has been named after Jesus.

Men and Women Are Equal in All Respects

In Islam men and women are equal in all respects, spiritually and otherwise. They are responsible for their actions. Men and women are protectors of each other. They enjoin what is good and forbid what is abominable. Both observe prayers and give charity and obey God and God's messenger. Both are entitled equally to God's mercy.

**Muslim men and women, believing men and women
Devout men and women, truthful men and women
Men and women who are patient and constant
Men and women who give in charity, men and women who fast
Men and women who guard their chastity
Men and women who remember God a lot
For them God has prepared forgiveness and a magnificent reward.
33:35**

**And if any do good deeds whether male or female
And have faith then they will enter the garden
And no injustice will be done to them. 4:124**

**The men who give charity and women who give charity
Are advancing a good loan to God.
It will be multiplied for them and they will have a generous reward.
57:18**

**God has promised men and women who believe
Gardens with streams of running water where they will abide forever.
In beautiful mansions in the Garden of Eden
And the blessings of God above all. That will be happiness supreme.
9:72**

Whoever does evil will be requited in accordance with it
But whoever does right, whether man or woman will enter paradise
Where they will have provision in abundance. 40:40p
However, there is one exception.
Men are the protectors and maintainers of women.
Because God has given the one more than the other
And because they support them from their means.
Therefore the righteous women are devoutly obedient, and guard
In the husband's absence what God would have them guard. 4:34p

The question here is what happens when a woman earns and helps the husband in the maintenance of the household, or as sometimes happens, she is the sole bread earner? In this case, does the wife enjoy equality or superiority over her husband?

To men is allotted what they earn and to women what they earn. 4:32p

This verse permits women to earn and to keep the earning to themselves. This verse may be read in conjunction with the dress regulations. If women go out to earn, they have to be dressed according to the fashion of the time and the demands of the job.

Share in Inheritance

We have appointed heirs for everything
That parents and close relatives leave behind,
Including those to whom you have pledged
Your hand in marriage, so give them their share.
God is witness to everything. 4:33

Men and women have a share
In what the parents and close relatives leave behind at death.
Whether the property be small or large-a determinate share. 4:7

Give to women their dowries as a gift,
But if they forego part of it themselves then use it to your advantage. 4:4

Fornication-Equal Punishment

In case of fornication, equal punishment is assigned to both man and woman.

The adulterer and the adulteress
Are each to be whipped a hundred strokes. 24:2p

As for those who accuse chaste women, but fail to produce four witnesses,
Whip them eighty strokes and never take testimony from them ever. 24:4p

It is thus next to impossible to prove adultery which requires the testimony of four eye witnesses.

If a husband accuses his wife of adultery without any witnesses, the testimony of the wife prevails over the testimony of her husband.

As for those who accuse their own wives
Without any witnesses but themselves,
Let the evidence of one of them be given four times,
Testifying in the name of God that he is telling the truth,
With the fifth affirmation being that God shall curse him if he is lying.
But it would ward off the penalty from her if she testifies in the name of God
That he is in fact lying-with the fifth affirmation being
That God should be angry at her if he is telling the truth. 24:6-9

The following verses are also relevant.

If any of your women are guilty of lewdness
Call for evidence against them from four of you.
If they give evidence confirming it,
Then keep them in houses until death claims them,
Or God makes a way for them. 4:15
If you fear disloyalty or ill conduct on the part of your women
Admonish them, then leave them alone in their beds,
Then spank them. If they mend, seek no means against them. 4:34p

Ms. Laleh Bakhtiar, a Muslim scholar of classic Arabic, who also has the distinction of having translated THE SUBLIME QURA'N into the English language, renders the entire verse (4:34) as follows:

Men are supporters of wives because God has given
Some of them an advantage over others
And because they spent of their wealth.
So the ones in accord with morality
Are the ones who are morally obligated
And the ones who guard the unseen
Of what God has kept safe.
And those women whose resistance you fear,
Admonish them and abandon them in their sleeping places
<u>And go away from them</u>. Then if they obey you,
Do not look for any way against them. 4:34

Thus the injunction that women who resist their husbands be spanked becomes controversial and is not universally accepted by Muslims.

<u>Dress Regulation</u>

Dress regulation is another area which has been massively confused by Muslim scholars. Islam demands that both men and women be decently dressed and in accordance with the prevailing fashion of the societies in which they are living.

Tell the believing men to lower their eyes and guard their private
parts.
Tell the believing women to lower their eyes and guard their private
parts,
And not to display their ornaments except the obvious ones,
And they should not strike their feet
In order to draw attention to their hidden ornaments
And to draw their coverings over their breasts
And not show their graces except to their husbands and their fathers
Or male attendants, free of sexual desires, or very young children
Who do not yet know the nakedness of women. 24:31p

O Prophet, tell your wives, your daughters, and the believing women
To put on their outer garments; that is most convenient
So they will be recognized and not molested. 33:59

To paraphrase the following are the Qura'nic injunctions on women's dress etiquette:

  a. Cover your bosoms in the society of males whom women are eligible to marry.
  b. When you step out of your homes, your dress and behavior should not be conspicuous in any way. Dress modestly and in accordance with the prevailing fashion. This will avoid the attention of those with sickness in their hearts and you will escape molestation.

In today's Western societies, Muslim women should avoid wearing "hijab" (covering of the head) or "burqa" (a one piece covering hiding the whole body) which identifies them as Muslims and which might cause them to be molested.

So why all this fuss about hijab and burqa? This insistence is against the spirit of the **Qurán** on women's dress code. Why are the Muslims insisting on defining their identity by the way their women dress? Why are the males not observing the Qura'nic injunction to keep their eyes lowered when on the street?

The **Qurán** contains more than 6,200 verses. Of these, only three regulate women's dress. On the other hand, more than a thousand verses emphasize the importance of knowledge and learning (Ilm.) About a hundred verses exhort mankind to be charitable, to help the needy and the orphan etc. More than one hundred verses ask you to respect other faiths and their followers. You are called upon to take care of the needy neighbors. All this irrespective of color, creed, or nationality. Thus education, charity, volunteerism, kind and courteous behavior toward all should be the hallmarks identifying the believers, according to the **Qurán**. For further details you may go through Chapters, 2, 3, and 4 once again.

Multiple Marriages

Multiple marriages is another area which has caused misunderstanding among Muslims and non-Muslims alike. Here again, Muslim clerics are entirely to blame for this impression. The **Qurán** does permit multiple marriages, conditionally.

If you fear that you cannot do justice by the orphans,
Marry women of your choice two, or three, or four,
But if you fear that you shall not be able to deal with them equitably,
Then marry only one. 4:3p

The **Qurán** further makes it clear that:

You are never able to do justice between wives,
Even if it is your ardent desire. 4:129p

Do these injunctions allow Muslim men to practice polygamy? The Muslim scholars who authorize polygamy are amending or overruling the **Qurán** and this smacks of blasphemy.

Thus, permission to marry more than one wife is allowed only when a man is burdened with the responsibility of rearing the orphans. The second condition is that he should deal with his wives justly and equitably. But the **Qurán** avers unequivocally that a man will never be able to treat all wives equitably, even if it is his ardent desire. So stick with one wife.

Right to Separation

Contrary to the impression widely prevailing, **Qurán** gives the women the right to separation.

If a woman fears abuse or desertion from her husband
There is no blame on them if they make a peaceful settlement
For peace is best. But men keep self-interest uppermost
If you two reconcile and are conscientious God is most merciful
But if they separate God will provide for each from the divine
abundance.
God is infinite in capacity, most judicious. 4:128-130

Rights of the Divorced Women

**And there is a fair support for divorced women
This is incumbent upon the righteous. 2:241**

Divorced women

**Are not permitted to conceal what God has created in their wombs
And their husbands have the right to take them back in that period,
if they wish to reconcile. And women shall have rights
Similar to the rights against them according to what is equitable
But men have a rank above them. 2:228p**

And give them their dowries as a gift. 4:44p

**When you have divorced your wives
And they have reached the end of the waiting period
Then keep them honorably (by revoking their divorce)
Or let them go with honor.
Do not take them back to injure them or to take undue advantage.
If anyone does that he wrongs his own soul,
Do not treat God's decrees as a jest. 2:231p**

**O prophet, when you divorce women, divorce them at their waiting
periods,
Be conscious of God, your Lord; do not expel them from their
houses
Nor let them leave unless they are openly immoral. 65:1p**

**When they have completed their appointed term,
Either keep them honorably or part with them honorably
God will provide for them from unexpected sources
God has set a due measure for everything. 65:2**

Thus the **Qurán's** concern for the divorced women is deep.

One Male Witness is Equal to Two Female Witnesses

**Believers, when you negotiate a debt for a fixed term
Draw up an agreement in writing.
It is better to have a scribe write down faithfully**

What the borrower dictates without leaving out a thing
But if the liable one is incompetent or infirm, or cannot dictate
Let his guardian dictate, honestly. And get the witness of two
witnesses
From your men; or if there are not two men,
Then a man and two women of your choice
So that if one of them errs the other may remind her. 2:282p

To draw the conclusion from this that one man is equal to two females in all aspects of life is going beyond the Qura'nic stipulation. This conditionality is restricted only to financial transactions in which the exposure of women is limited and may lead to forgetfulness or confusion. It is therefore necessary to have another woman to prompt the first witness if she forgets or is confused. As has been repeatedly pointed out, men and women are equal in all spheres of activity. They are honorable members of society, in no way inferior to men. So Muslim women stand up and demand the rights given to you by God, whether it is dress regulation, right to divorce, share in inheritance, or the right to work to earn etc.

Chapter Eight

QURÁN AND JIHAD

Victims of aggression are given permission to fight because injustice has been done to them.
And God is well able to help those-
Who were driven away from their homes for no other Reason than their saying,
"Our Lord is God."   22:39, 40p

Fight in God's cause against those who wage war against you, but do not commit aggression-for verily God does not love aggressors. 2:190

Chapter 8

Qurán and Jihad

Jihad is a much misunderstood and much maligned word in the West. Historically also, this concept is blamed for all the ills the West found unsavory in Islam and is blamed for the present conflict between the West and some Muslim countries. Jihad is seen as a holy war waged by Muslims on non-Muslims to subdue them or to convert them to Islam. These insinuations are more deliberate than inadvertent. This is so even today as discussed in some detail in the Introduction.

Islam definitely is not a meek religion. It prescribes slapping back the fellow who slaps you, but do not be the first to slap. And the best course is to forgive the slapper. Fight those who wage war against you, but do not commit aggression. God does not love the aggressor. Victims of aggression are permitted to fight because injustice has been done to them. Jihad against oppression, strife, and persecution is obligatory, as it is against hypocrites and atheists. Atheists fight for the powers of evil and believers fight in the way of God. Fight the infidels, those who by-pass the divine law.

Jihad has many aspects. "Jihad has many facets and is fought on all fronts, spiritual, political, social, personal, military and economic," says Karen Armstrong, an eminent scholar of major religions including Buddhism, in her book THE BATTLE FOR GOD, Chapter 2, "Muslims the Conservative Spirit 1492-1799."

Jihad means striving after, an internal struggle-struggle to live in peace and harmony with himself. Man gets nothing but what he strives for. The fruit of this striving will soon come in sight and he will be rewarded with a complete reward, so says the **Qurán** and this is the primary aspect of jihad. To God is the final goal. Life is sacred, do not take life which God has made sacred except by way of justice and law. This way man will learn wisdom.

Whatever Jihad is, it is definitely not a battle against other faiths; neither is it a battle between the Muslims and the West. As has been made clear in Chapter 1, there is no proselytizing in Islam. It is only an invitation. How could it be otherwise? Islam's God is God of all mankind. The **Qurán** is a book of guidance and mercy to all mankind. Muhammad has been sent as a mercy to all mankind. All these aspects have been exhaustively dealt with in chapters 1, 2, 3, and 5. These need not be repeated except a few.

We gave Moses the book as a mercy. 6:154

We gave Jesus, son of Mary the gospel with guidance and truth in it. 5:46p

We sent Jesus, son of Mary with the gospel
And we ordained in the hearts of those who followed him
Compassion and mercy. 57:27p

And this Qurán is the book which we have revealed as a blessing,
So follow it and be righteous that you may receive mercy. 6:155

Say, "We believe in God and the revelation given to us,
And to Abraham, Ismael, Isaac, Jacob, and the Tribes
And that given to Moses and Jesus and that given to all prophets
from their Lord.
We make no difference between one and the other of them
And we submit to God." 21:36

And say, "I believe in any scripture that God has revealed.
And I have been commanded to treat you all justly.
God is our Lord and your Lord too.
We are responsible for our acts, and you for your acts.
Let there be no argument between us.
God will unite us, and to Him is the final goal." 42:15p

The Muslims, the Jews, the Christians and the Sabians
Who believe in God and the last day and are righteous

Have their reward with their Lord.
There is nothing for them to fear; nor shall they sorrow. 2:62

For each of them (refers to followers of all faiths)
We have established a law, and a revealed way. 5:48p

In the light of the above verses, how could Muslims wage a war against Jews or Christians or people of other faiths?

The **Qurán** looks upon war as undesirable. The book enjoins its followers to use all the means at their command to end a war, if waged, at the earliest and restore peace. Nowhere does it sanctify aggressive war. The **Qurán** condemns wanton killing and aggression. Fight those who fight you, but do not transgress limits. God does not love transgressors. If the enemy ceases to fight, hostility must come to an end and guarantees of peace must be sent out.

The Qura'nic authority for what has been said and more on Jihad follows.

Victims of aggression are given permission to fight because
Injustice has been done to them.
And God is well able to help those-
Who were driven away from their homes for no other
Reason than their saying, "Our Lord is God." 22:39, 40p

So fight in the way of God. You are only in charge of yourself,
But urge the believers to fight,
It may well be that God will keep back the might of the infidels
For God's might is greater and more severe in punishment. 4:84

The infidels should not think that they can bypass (the law of God)
Surely they cannot get away.
Prepare against them whatever arms and cavalry
You can muster, that you may strike terror
In (the hearts of) the enemies of God and your own,
And others besides them not known to you, but known to God.
But if they are inclined to peace, make peace with them,
And have trust in God for He hears all and knows everything.
8:59-60p, 61

A general proclamation is (made) this day of the Greater Pilgrimage
On the part of God and His Apostle,
That God is not bound (by any contract) to idolaters, nor is His
Apostle.
It is, therefore, better for you to repent.
If you do not, remember that you cannot elude (the grip) of God.
So announce to those who deny the truth the news of painful
punishment
Except those idolaters with whom you have a treaty,
Who have not failed you in the least, not helped anyone against you.
Fulfill your obligations to them during the term (of the treaty).
God loves those who take heed for themselves
But when these months, prohibited (for fighting) are over,
Slay the idolaters wherever you find them,
And take them captive or besiege them,
And lie in wait for them at every likely place
If they repent and fulfill their devotional obligations
And pay the zakat, then let them go their way,
For God is forgiving and kind. 9:3-5

Fight those people of the Book who do not believe
In God and the Last Day, who do not prohibit what God
And His Apostle have forbidden, nor accept divine law,
Until all of them pay the protective tax (jizya) in submission. 9:29

O Prophet, strive against the atheists and the hypocrites,
And be hard on them; their abode is hell;
And what a miserable destination! 9:73 and 66:9

Believers, fight the atheists near you, and let them find severity
in you
And know that God is with the conscientious. 9:123

So, when you clash with the unbelievers,
Smite their necks until you overpower them,
Then hold them in bondage. Then either free them graciously
Or after taking a ransom, until war shall have come to end. 47:4p

Fighting is prescribed for you, even if it is abhorrent to you.
It may be that you dislike something that is good for you,
And it may be that you like something that is bad for you
God knows and you do not know. 2:216

Believers fight in the way of God while atheists fight for the sake
of idols;
So fight the friends of Satan for the strategy of Satan is weak. 4:7

They ask you about fighting in the sacred months.
Say, "Fighting in them is an atrocity
But more atrocious to God is blocking the way to the path of God
Denying God, preventing access to the sacred mosque
And driving out its people, and persecution is worse than killing.
2:217p

And do not consider those killed in God's cause to be dead;
No, they are alive, being supported in the presence of their Lord.
3:169

So let those who trade the life of this world for the hereafter
Fight in the cause of God. Whoever fights in the cause of God,
Whether slain or victorious, we will give a tremendous reward
What has come upon you that you fight not in the cause of God
And for the oppressed, men, women, and children, who pray:
"Get us out of this city, O Lord whose people are oppressors
So send us a friend by Your will, and send us a helper." 4:73-5

Forced Conversion by Way of Jihad

This aspect has already been covered in detail in Chapter 1. I will quote
again some important verses.

Let there be no compulsion in religion:
Truth stands out clear from error. 2:256p

We have revealed the Book to you in truth for mankind
He that receives guidance benefits his own soul
But he that strays injures his own soul.
You are not set a custodian over them. 39:41

And to rehearse the Qurán, and if any accept guidance
They do it for the good of their own souls
And if any stray, say, "I'm only a warner." 27:92

Invite to the way of your Lord with wisdom and good advice,
And debate with others in the most dignified manner. 16:125p

"Whoever heeds the messenger is being obedient to God,
As for those who turn away, we have not sent you as a guard over
them" 4:80

Insights from you Lord have already come to you: So if anyone sees,
It is for his own benefit; and if anyone is blind, that will be his loss.
And say I am not a guardian to watch over you. 6:104

Had He willed they would not have been idolaters.
We have not appointed you their guardian, nor are you their
pleader. 6:107

If they accuse you of falsehood, say, "My work to me, and your
work to you.
You are not responsible for what I do,
And I am not responsible for what you do." 10:41
Say, "Obey God and obey the Apostle, but if you turn away,
Then for him is his duty to fulfill, and for you the burden that you
carry;
Yet if you obey him you will be rightly guided.
The duty of the Messenger is to convey the message clearly." 24:54

And to recite the Qurán whoever comes to guidance does so for himself;
As for him who strays, tell him "I am only a warner." 27:92

And do not contest the people of scripture, unless with what is better,
Except those of them who have been unjust;
Say, 'We believe in what was revealed to us, in what was revealed
to you,
For our God and your God is one, to Whom we submit." 29:46

We have sent down this Book to you with the truth for all mankind.
So, he who comes to guidance does so for himself,

And he who goes astray does so for his own loss;
On you does not lie their guardianship. 39:41

So then give the call, and be upright as you have been commanded,
Not following their wishes.
And say, "I believe in any scripture that God has revealed.
And I have been commanded to treat all of you fairly
God is our Lord and your Lord too.
We are responsible for our acts, and you are responsible for your acts.
Let there be no argument between us.
God will unite us, and the journey is to God." 42:15

So if they turn away, we have not sent you as a guard over them:
Your only obligation is communication.
Whenever we let man taste mercy from Us, he rejoices in it,
But when ill befalls him because of what he himself has brought
about,
Then man is a faithless ingrate indeed." 42:48
Say, "O atheists I don't serve what you serve
And you don't serve what I serve
You have your way and I have my way." 109:1-2, 6

Is this conversion by force?

So let us leave the current but recurring, misguided definition of Jihad to political leaders who have political axes to grind, and to Muslim Jihadists who are misguided, and the former pope, Pope Benedict XVI, who sees in Islam a major obstacle to his mission. In his commitment to revive and propagate Christianity, he quotes with approval a fourteenth century obscure Byzantine Emperor, Emperor Manual II who is reported to have seen in Islam only evil. This the pope did in his address at a German university delivered on September 20, 2006. He further vilified Islam by asserting that Islam's "God commands the irrational and the will to dominate." The church, even today, assigns supernatural powers to some of its followers, beatifies them and confers on them the nimbus of sainthood, thus assigning them a status equal to Jesus Christ. Miracle workers have always been set up as important tools of evangelism. Is this rational? The pope momentarily appears to be unmindful of what the Vatican Ecumenical Council conceded in 1962, that "Islam has given mankind important truths about God, Jesus, and the prophets." One can always cite somebody or another to support one's inclinations. For example, I can also quote Gallio, a provincial Roman governor, who asked: "Can any good thing come out of Nazareth?"

Those who are interested in knowing the Islamic Jihad may read with profit the book DEFEATING THE JIHADISTS. A BLUEPRINT FOR ACTION authored by Richard A. Clark and others.

Chapter Nine

Qurán and Terrorism

Your Lord forbids you from killing a person
Which God has made sacred
Except by way of justice and Law. 6:151p
We have sent you (Muhammad) as a mercy
to all peoples 21:107

Since the end of time is sure to come
Overlook any human faults with gracious forgiveness.   15:85p

Chapter 9

Qurán and Terrorism

Terrorism is defined as the killing of civilians who are in no way involved in war or conflict. It is indiscriminant killing of innocent civilians with the object of creating terror and fear in the targeted society in retaliation for some perceived wrong. If we agree with this definition, then terrorism is totally alien to Islam. It amounts to rejecting the faith. **Qurán** is a book for all mankind. Every human being carries within him the divine spirit and is to be treated with respect and kindness.

Now terrorism against whom? The Christians, the Jews, the Sabians, the Zoroastrians, the Buddhists, the Hindus, or members of any other creed, or sect or religion? Let me quote what the **Qurán** has to say about these religions.

As for the Muslims, the Jews, the Sabians,
The Christians, the Magians, and the polytheists,
God will decide among them on the day of resurrection.
For God is witness to all things. 22:17

For the ancient religions of the Indian subcontinent, please go to Chapter 5 which may be read in conjunction with Chapter 9. This will avoid repetition of many verses.

The Muslims, the Jews, the Christians, and the Sabians,
Who believe in God and the last day and do good
Have their reward with their Lord.
There is nothing for them to fear or grieve. 2:62

Come and I will declare what your Lord has forbidden you.
You should not associate anything with God;
You should be good to your parents,
And not kill your children on account of poverty,
We provide for you and for them
And do not approach indecencies whether outward or inward.
And do not kill a person which God has made sacred-except by justice.
Thus God commands you, so that you may understand. 6:151p

We gave Moses the scripture as guidance and mercy. 6:154p

Qurán is a blessed book which we have revealed;
So follow it and be conscientious that you may receive mercy. 6:155

Pray to your Lord humbly and secretly
For God does not love the aggressive. 7:55

And do not cause trouble after order has been established. 7:56p

So when the Qurán is recited listen to it silently,
That you may experience mercy. 7:204

And if you inflict punishment,
Then inflict punishment equivalent to the vengeance wrought on you:
But if you are patient that is certainly the best" 16:1-2, 6p
Do not take a life that God has made sacred, except for just cause.
And if anyone is killed unjustly, we have given his heir authority;
To demand qisas (blood money) or to forgive:
But let him not exceed bounds in the matter of taking life
For he is helped by the law. 17:33

We have sent you (Muhammad)only as a mercy to all peoples. 21:107

For if God did not parry people by means of one another,
Then monasteries and churches and synagogues and mosques
Wherein the name of God is much recited would surely be demolished. 22:40p

Do not forget your part in this world.
And be good, as God has been good to you.
And do not seek corruption on earth,
For God does not love the corrupt. 28:77

These are the signs of the Book full of wisdom,
Guidance and mercy for those who do good,
Those who pray regularly and give alms
And who are certain of the hereafter
They are following guidance from their Lord
And they are the ones who thrive 31:2-5

O prophet, we have sent you as witness, a herald, and a warner;
And one who invites to God by divine leave and an illuminating
lamp. 33:45-6

God has prescribed for you what God enjoined on Noah,
By which we inspired you, and what we enjoined
On Abraham, Moses, and Jesus,
That you may be steadfast in faith and not be disunited in it. 42:13p

Invite to the way of your Lord with wisdom and good advice,
And debate with others in the most dignified manner. 16:125p

Light from God has come to you, a clear Book,
By which God guides those who follow divine will
To ways of peace and safety
And brings them from darkness into light. 5:15p-16p

And We only created the heavens and the earth
And everything in between them for just ends
And since the end of time is sure to come,
When this will be manifest
So overlook any human faults with gracious forgiveness. 15:85

Please go through all this and the whole book and you will agree
with me that Islam and terrorism are antithetical. Let us recall that
Qurán is a book of guidance and mercy for all mankind and so is
Islamic God-God of all the world.

Look at the world today (2013) Muslims are killing Muslims. Muslims are the target of terrorism waged by their fellow Muslims. There is a strife and conflict and civil war in many Muslim countries. So what is the West's concern?

Chapter Ten

JUSTICE

*When you judge between man and man you should judge with
justice. 4:58p
Whoever intercedes for good has a share in it
And whoever helps an evil cause shares in its burden. 4:85p
Believers stand out firmly for God as witnesses for justice
And let not the hatred of others
Make you swerve to wrong and depart from justice.
Be just, that is next to piety. 5:8p
Believers stand out firmly for justice, as witnesses to God,
Even be it against yourselves or your parents or relatives;
Whether one be rich or poor, God is closer and more worthy than
either.
And do not follow desire lest you swerve from justice
And if you pervert it or neglect it, God is aware of what you do.
4:135*

*And do not kill a person which God has made sacred
Except by way of justice and Law. 6:151p*

Chapter 10

Qurán and Justice

Justice according to law is another important pillar of Islamic state. A society which cannot enforce justice fully, quickly, and impartially according to the law of the land, is a failed state-on the way to extinction.

Mankind is asked to stand up firmly in support of justice and fair play. Do not follow the lusts or inclinations while dispensing justice. Do not decline to do justice. Do not pervert justice or neglect it. Islamic justice is justice tempered with mercy and forgiveness.

The imperatives of justice are high in Islam. In the West even today a person is exempt from testifying against his blood relations. This exemption is not available in Islam. One is bound to testify, even if it goes against oneself, the parents, or brothers and sisters, husbands and wives, rich or poor in furtherance of justice.

While deposing, please be warned that you are God's witness, so let not your hatred of others swerve you from the path of justice. God prohibits you from taking life without due process of law and without meeting the demands of justice. Whenever you speak, speak justly. The prophet says that my God has commanded justice. Justice is next to piety. Justice is the supreme criterion by which your souls will be judged on the day of accountability. On that day, no outside intercession will be accepted, nor any compensation. The only intercession is God's mercy and forgiveness. Justice tempered with mercy and forgiveness are the guiding principles. You are forbidden to try to influence the judges or bribe them to get a verdict in your favor. Do not use your wealth as a bait to the judges. When one is arbitrating he should be just and fair.

In the end judgment and justice will come to pass. 55:7-9
God is the best of judges. 6:57p

The Qura'nic authority for what has been said is now quoted.

God demands you to render back your trust
To those to whom they are due
And when you judge between man and man
You should judge with justice
How excellent is the teaching which God gives you. 4:58p

Believers stand out firmly for justice, as witnesses to God,
Even be it against yourselves or your parents or relatives;
Whether one be rich or poor, God is closer and more worthy than
either.
And do not follow desire lest you swerve from justice
And if you pervert it or neglect it, God is aware of what you do.
4:135

God does not compel a soul to do what is beyond its ability;
One gets what one has earned
And is responsible for what one deserves. 2:286p

Say, "My Lord has commanded justice." 7:181

Believers stand out firmly for God as witnesses for justice
And let not the hatred of others
Make you swerve to wrong and depart from justice.
Be just, that is next to piety. 5:8p

Come, and I will declare what your Lord has forbidden you.
You should not associate anything with God-
You should be good to your parents
And not kill your children on account of poverty
We provide for you and for them
And do not kill a person which God has made sacred
Except by justice; thus God commands you that you may
understand. 6:151p

And give full weight and measure, with justice to go
We do not burden any soul beyond its capacity.
So when you speak, be just even if it concerns a close relative.
God thus commands you so you may be mindful. 6:152p

He that does good shall have ten times as much to his credit:
He that does evil shall only be compensated according to his evil
No wrong shall be done to anyone. 6:160

Every soul draws the meed of its acts on none but itself
No bearer of burdens can bear the burden of another
Your goal in the end is to God. 6:164p

The balance that Day will be true
Those whose scale of good is heavy will prosper
Those whose scale is light will find their souls in perdition,
For wrongfully treating our signs. 7:8-9

Say, "O my people, give just measure and weight.
Do not withhold from the people the things that are their due."
11:85p

God sets another parable of two men-one of them dumb with no power,
A wearisome burden on his master.
Is such a man equal with one who commands justice
And is on a straight way? 16:76p

God commands justice,
The doing of good and liberality to kith and kin
He forbids all shameful deeds, and injustice and rebellion
He instructs you that you may receive admonition. 16:90

We shall set up scales of justice for the Day of Judgment
So that no soul will be dealt with unjustly in the least. 21:47p

If any does good the reward to him is better than his deed,
But if any does evil the doers of evil are
Only punished to the extent of their deeds. 28:84

Then on that Day not a soul will be wronged in the least
And you shall be repaid the meeds of your past deeds. 36:54

But there is no cause against those who defend after being oppressed
There is cause against those who oppress people
And wreak injustice in the land, without right;
For them there is a painful penalty yet if anyone is patient and forgives
That is a determination that will resolve affairs. 42:41-3

To all are assigned degrees according to the deeds which they have done
In order that God may recompense their deeds
And no injustice be done to them. 46:19
If two parties among the believers fall into a quarrel
Make peace between them with justice and be fair.
God loves those who are just. 49:9p

Verily, judgment and justice must indeed come to pass. 51:6

God is the best of judges. 6:57p

On the Day of Judgment men will proceed in companies sorted out;
To be shown the deeds that they had done
Then shall anyone who has done an atom's weight of good, see it.
And anyone who has done an atom's weight of evil, shall see it. 99:6-8

On the Day whose balance of good deeds is found heavy
Will be in a life of good pleasure and satisfaction
But he whose balance of good deeds is found to be light
Will have his home in a pit. 101:6-9

Whoever intercedes for good has a share in it
And whoever helps an evil cause shares in its burden 4:85p

Chapter Eleven

THE QURA'NIC PHILOSOPHY
OF HISTORY

These are some of the stories of the communities We relate
to you.
Of them, some are standing and some have been mown down.
We did not wrong them. They wronged their own souls.   11:100
No people can hasten their term nor can they delay it.   24:43
No community will be destroyed for a single wrong doing, if its
members are likely to mend.   11:117
The people of Lut rejected the messenger.
And transgressed all limits.
Thus disrupting the way of nature.
And We destroyed them   26:165p,166p, and 27-28,29p

Chapter 11

The Qura'nic Philosophy of History

History confers significance to events in time. The historians' task is to distinguish between the significant, the trivial, and the accidental. History is a narration of man's development and his achievements in various fields of activity such as science, religion, politics, law and justice, the economic activities, the state of the government, of morality, of the military, as well as the social structure of the times.

Initially, and for a long time, history was a record of the "noble" exploits of the priests, the monarchs, the emperors, and the conquering generals. It was written by the victor to glorify himself and to demonize the vanquished.

Ibn-e-Khaldun (1332-1406 CE) was the first historian to look at history as a composite whole-as a study of a civilization, a record of a nation's political, economic, scientific, religious, educational, military, moral, and artistic activities at a given time. He also studied the relationship between politics and religion. To him, the way history was being written until then was worthless. He is the trail blazer historian who changed forever the direction of the way history was being written. Arnold J. Toynbee (1889-1975 CE) the Nobel laureate in history, and the greatest historian of civilizations called Ibn-e-Khaldun "the most illuminating interpreter of the history of morphology that has appeared in the world so far," and "as the outstanding genius in the field of the study of morphology of history."

Inspired by Ibn-e-Khaldun the later historians have interpreted history in different ways.

History for one school is the manifestation of the divine providence, a drama of God's will. Every important event is a lesson taught by heaven to man. Man is a helpless spectator, a passive being unable to influence the course of history.

For another school, geography is the major player, influencing human development. Climate, soil, rainfall, rivers, coastlines, and environment are the factors which determine the destiny of a nation.

And yet another school believes that race is the determining factor in the rise and fall of nations. Science, art, and all that is noble and great in a civilization springs from the white race, the Teutonic, the Nordic, the Anglo-Saxons. The brown or the yellow or black races are inferior and incapable of leaving a mark in history.

These three viewpoints however, stand discredited.

For Thomas Carlyle, the universal history of what man has accomplished is at bottom the deeds of the great minds, the geniuses, the heroes, the prophets, the discoverers, the inventors, and the creators in various fields of human activity. They are the minds who move forward the human civilization. The prophet, the philosopher, and the sage are the instructors of mankind.

For one school, the basic influence in human history is the economic activity; the mode of production and distribution of wealth, its division and consumption, the relationship of the employer and the employee- and the class war between the handful of bourgeoisie and the vast proletariat, ending ultimately in the victory of the proletariat and the establishment of a classless society. This school was a reaction to the inhuman exploitation of the labor by the capitalists, the founders of industry in the initial stages of the Industrial Revolution. Founded by Karl Marx, it found its home in the USSR after the 1917 revolution. After a phenomenal rise in the post-World War II era, it collapsed with the disintegration of the Soviet Union in 1990. In China also which is another country following Marxian socialism, this philosophy is being gradually eroded.

A German historian has advanced the proposition that human civilizations are born, grow, reach their pinnacle, and decline and die like a human being. History moves in a cycle and external factors have little bearing on the course of history. This interpretation is fatalistic and man as a player has no significance. So far, the weight of history has borne this interpretation.

Toynbee, the greatest historian of civilization, on the other hand, is of the view that history need not move in a cycle and could be made to move linearly. In his view, civilizations decline and die because the men that matter are unable to see the challenges which a civilization in decline faces. Should the malaise be detected in time and effectively responded, there is no reason for a civilization to die. If this happens, civilization will move in a straight line and advance forward continuously. This approach defies the evidence of history and is yet to be tested. It may well turn out to be a wish Toynbee is reading into history.

The Qura'nic Philosophy of History

The Qura'nic outlook is simple. God has sent his messengers to many nations, communities, tribes etc. as the guides and philosophers of their communities. Most communities rejected their prophets and fell. In some cases, people followed their prophets and prospered, but their descendants deviated from the way of their forefathers and perished. The universal message these prophets brought to their communities is contained in the following paraphrase of the verses.

God sent to the Madayan people Shuayab, one of them as a messenger. His teaching was:

Worship God. You have no other God but Him. Give just measure and weight. Do not withhold from the people the things that are their due and establish justice. Do not commit evil in the land with intent to do mischief.

But his people rejected him and a mighty blast seized them and they lay prostrate in their homes in the morning, as if they had never lived and flourished. Shuayab and those who believed in him were saved. Paraphrase **11:84-5, 94p-95**

Such was the fate of most communities.

These are some of the stories of the communities We relate to you.
Of them, some are standing and some have been mown down.
We did not wrong them. They wronged their own souls.
The deities whom they invoked did not profit them a bit. 11:100-101p

The people of Noah rejected him and we drowned them.
Such is the penalty for the wrongdoers. 25:37p

The people of Lut rejected the messenger.
Leaving aside their females, they approached males

And transgressed all limits. So we rained down on them
A shower of brimstones. 24:165p-166p

Remember Ad and Thamud and Qarun, Pharoah, Haman.
They behaved with insolence on the earth
Each one of them was seized for his crime.
Against some we sent a violent tornado,
Some were caught by a blast, some we caused the earth to swallow,
And some we drowned. It was not God who injured them.
They injured their own souls. 69:1-10

I will now list some of the sins the **Qurán** mentions as responsible
for the fall of civilizations outside of those highlighted by their prophets.

When any community in power fails:
  a. To eliminate fear and uncertainty
  b. To establish peace and security
  c. To enforce rule of law and justice
  d. To establish social justice to eliminate poverty, want, and hunger
  e. To possess a majority of persons of balanced good sense; instead
      the majority consisted of sinners and wrongdoers
  f. To eliminate corruption on earth is doomed to extinction.

These were the people given to contention. 19:97p

God has promised to those among you who believe
And work righteous deeds inheritance (of power) in the land
As He granted it to those before them
So if they are established in authority,
And will change the state of fear in which they lived
To one of security and peace. 24:55p paraphrased

Many were the communities we utterly destroyed
Because they were unjust and
We set up other communities in their place. 21:11

Rejection of God's signs is another major cause of the downfall of
civilizations.

We sent messengers before you to their respective peoples.
And they came to them with clear signs
Then to those who transgressed, we meted out retribution.
And it was due from Us to aid those who believed. 22:47

The companions of the Rocky Tract also rejected the messengers.
We sent them our signs but they persisted in turning away from
them
They had hewn their edifices in mountains, feeling secure
But a mighty blast seized them of a morning
What all they did with such art and care was of no avail to them.
15:80-84

The people of Ad continued to reject our signs
And behaved arrogantly throughout the land against truth and
reason
So we sent them a furious wind through days of disaster
To give them a taste of a penalty of humiliation paraphrase of
41:15p-16p

There are about fifteen verses on the same subject.

The stories of the prophets are also "signs" narrated for mankind
to learn lessons from them. (For a definition of "signs" of God, please
see Chapter 4.)

You are among those invited to spend in the way of God.
But some among you are misers and they are so
At the expense of their own souls.
God is free of all needs and you are the needy.
If you turn back God will substitute in your stead
Another people who will not be misers. 47:38

Having said all this, the **Qurán** repeatedly asks man to travel
through the earth and see how the past civilizations passed away and how
God raised other generations after them. There is a close relationship
between history and archaeology. The ruins of past civilizations speak
no words, but their remains powerfully bond us to a past that continues
to have deep meaning for today's world. Hence, the Qura'nic insistence

on study of archaeology to discover the deeds and misdeeds which destroyed civilizations. The lessons thus learned should inform man's present activities and provide guidelines for the future.

Many were the ways of life that have passed away before you:
Travel through the earth and see what was the end of those
Who rejected truth. 3:137 and 6:11

How many populations have we destroyed which were being unjust
They tumbled down on their roofs.
And how many wells lie abandoned and castles lofty and well-built
Do they not travel through the land so that their hearts and minds
may learn wisdom and their ears learn to hear?
Truly it is not their eyes that are blind but their hearts
Which are in their breasts. 22:45-6

Haven't they traveled the earth and seen
How many of those before them ended up?
They were more powerful than these and they plowed the land
And populated it more than these have peopled it. 30:9p

Say, "Travel the earth and see how those before you ended up;
Do they not travel through the earth and see what was
The end of those before them?
They were superior to them in strength:
They tilled the soil and populated in greater numbers
Than these have done. There came to them their messengers
With clear signs which they rejected to their own destruction
It was not God who wronged them
But they wronged their own souls. 30:9 and 40:21

Say, "Travel through the earth and see what was the end
Of those before you. Most of them worshiped others
Besides God." 30:42

Do they not travel through the earth and see
What was the end of those before them?
They were more numerous than these and superior in strength
And in the traces they left in the land

Yet all that they accomplished was of no profit to them. 40:82

However, before God destroys a civilization, a warning is sent to them.

When We decide to destroy a population We send a definite order
To those among them who are given the good things of this life
And yet transgress so that the Word is proved true against them.
Then We annihilated them. 17:16

And Lut warned his people of their punishment
But they disputed about the warning
Early on the morrow an abiding punishment seized them. 54:36, 38

The Thamud also rejected their warners.
We sent against them a mighty blast and they became
Like the dried stubble used by one who pens cattle. 54:23 and 54:31

The **Qurán** also suggests that for all civilizations a term has been decreed and assigned beforehand. This would suggest the philosophy of history enunciated by Oswald Springler.

Nor did we destroy a population that had not a term decreed
And assigned beforehand.
A people can neither anticipate its term nor delay it.15:4-5
To every people is a term appointed: when their term is reached,
Not an hour can they cause delay, nor can they advance it by an
hour. 7:34

No people can hasten their term nor can they delay it. 23:43

The above verses are categorical in stating that the term of a civilization is fixed. Nonetheless, there is a promise of their lives being prolonged if they mend their ways.

As for those who repudiate our signs,
We will bring them to destruction without their even knowing
Yet I prolong their lives for My strategy is solid. 7:182-3

Had it not been for a word that went forth before from your Lord
The punishment must necessarily have come;

But there is a term appointed for respite. 20:1-9

**If God were to punish men according to what they deserve,
He would not leave on the back of the earth
A single living creature: but He gives them respite for a stated term
35:45p**

God also suggests that a single wrong doing by a community would not lead to its destruction provided the community mends its ways.

**Your Lord would not destroy a community for a single wrong doing
If its members are likely to mend 11:117**

Thus the door is always open to make amends and allow civilizations to move in a straight line.

Conclusion

The Qura'nic philosophy of history is simple. When you inherit power and want to survive and prosper, follow the messages of the prophets and the wise men amongst you, follow the signs of God, and avoid the mistakes that have been recounted in the **Qurán**. Carefully study the rise and fall of bygone civilizations, apply the lessons learned to your present conduct and future behavior, and mend your ways. This will invite God's mercy and may lead to the extension of a civilization's term.

Chapter Twelve

QURA'NIC GUIDELINES ON ECONOMICS

Riba(usuriousinterest)multipliedandcompoundedisforbidden. 3:130p and *275p*
Spend in charity whatever is beyond your needs   2:219p
Guard against avarice.   64:16p
Do not be niggardly. 4:37p
Do not be a spendthrift. 17:26p
Those who accumulate a hoard will face an agony that is inevitable. 70:18
In your wealth there is an acknowledged right for the poor and the marginalized. 70:24,5
Ensure that wealth does not circulate among the wealthy in your midst.   59:7p

Chapter 12

Qura'nic Guidelines on Economics

Like history, **Qurán** offers economic guidelines for mankind. It is unfortunate that this aspect, like so many areas of importance in Islamic polity which relate to life in this world, have been by-passed by the Muslim scholars. This, I believe, is so because of their ignorance of the subject. Their knowledge is confined to "riba" (usury.) If asked to define riba, they unequivocally state that riba is interest and forbidden. Little do they know that riba is not interest, it is usury, interest compounded many times. They are unaware of the complex role interest plays in today's economy. It protects your purchasing power against inflation, namely rising prices. The value of the money is in its purchasing power. If a shopkeeper refuses to exchange his goods for your paper or plastic money, it is worthless. Inflation in today's world is a fact of life. In Japan, the lending rate is zero per cent. Will you call this economy Islamic? This rate in the European Union, the United States, and other Western economies is very low, as low as one per cent. Will you call their economies very close to Islamic economy? The interest rate in Pakistan is fifteen per cent. In all Muslim counties, this rate varies from eight to ten per cent. Have the Muslim scholars condemned their economies as un-Islamic? Let me put it a little differently. I approach a well to do old friend of mine, a Muslim, for an interest free loan of one hundred thousand US dollars to purchase a small house with the stipulation that the amount will be paid back in five years. If you were the rich friend, will you agree to the loan in the face of inflation? No, because in five years the value of your money would have gone down and the value of the house the loanee had purchased would have gone up. This is very unfair to the lender. Interest free economy in an inflationary society will lead to collapse of the economic structure. The value of your money against inflation was protected under gold standard or where there is a barter economy. It could also be protected if the money loaned is expressed in terms of gold or a major commodity to be repaid with equal weight of gold or equal amount of the same commodity.

It is for this reason the **Qurán** defines riba not as simple interest, but as interest compounded, doubled, and multiplied (usury.) Riba is forbidden because it is usurpation of others' wealth unjustly. Those who consume usurious interest are in a business in which only those maddened by the devil's touch engage. Usury is greed and exploitation of the poor by the rich. It is immoral.

I now quote the Qura'nic authority for what has been stated.

Believers, do not consume riba(usurious interest) multiplied and compounded
And be conscious of God that you may prosper. 3:130

The Jews practiced usury although it had been forbidden them:
Riba (usury) is usurping other people's wealth unjustly. 4:161p

Those who consume usurious interest are in a business
In which only those maddened by the devil's touch engage.
That is because they say usury is like trade.
But God has permitted trade and forbidden usury. 2:275

Interest rates are also applied to control rising prices, to encourage people to save and invest and refrain from conspicuous consumption. An interest rate equal to the rate of inflation plus say four percent more to meet the bank's expenditure, to provide hedge against loan defaulters, as well as to leave a reasonable margin of profit for the bank is not usury. However, it should be the responsibility of the central bank of a country to determine the rate of interest allowed on bank borrowings.

In today's world, three philosophies of economy are being practiced, namely capitalism, Marxian socialism, and British socialism.

Capitalism is free economy left to the market forces to determine the direction of the economy. Government interference is least. This system is driven by a heartless profit motive-profit of the individual or the corporation with no conscience. Capitalism faces periodic ups and downs and inflation is a recurring feature. The present worldwide economic recession and hardships testify to its iniquitous nature. This system is currently (2013) facing serious problems, and because of this almost all countries of the world are facing economic recession, unemployment, etc. During the present crisis, governments practicing capitalism have interfered massively with the economy. It appears that this interference has come to stay. At the end of the day, a new system may emerge in the form of a diluted capitalism.

Then there is Marxian socialism. This economy is totally managed by the state. Free enterprise is not permitted. It is the responsibility of the state to ensure employment, free education, health, housing etc. to its citizens. An excellent system, but mismanagement led to its downfall. The Soviet Union and later China were the major practitioners of the system. With the disintegration of the Soviet Union, the system is no more. Its successor state, the Russian Republic, has reverted to capitalism. Even communist China is opening its door gradually to free enterprise in nominated areas.

The third system is British socialism. This is a happy medium between Marxian socialism and American capitalism. Free enterprise is the basic pillar of the system, but at the same time, the government imposes heavy taxes on all to provide a strong social network for the poor and to provide free education up to a level and free medical facilities. Subsidized transport and housing and unemployment allowance are the other important features of the system. Countries like Canada, Sweden, Norway, and Holland are the most successful practitioners of this system. If judged by Qura'nic standards, the economies of these countries are closest to Islamic economy. Islam allows free enterprise in all economic fields, but taxation is very, very heavy to insure social justice as well as to provide a strong social net to protect the indigent, as Islam and poverty do not go together.

Islam believes in social justice, total eradication of poverty, want, illiteracy and disease. In short, a welfare state. Islam allows free enterprise, but free from greed and extravagance. The whole system has a strong moral content. Wealth is God's trust. Be mindful of how you spend it. Islam exhorts shared prosperity. It is obligatory on all the well to do and the government to take full care of the poor, the needy, the widow, the orphan, the needy traveler, of those who are in need and yet do not ask out of shame. Seek out such people and help them. Muslims are called upon to help the neighbor in straitened circumstances. The poor have a recognized right in the wealth of the well to do. All enabled Muslims are directed to give out in charity. How much are they to give? Whatever is surplus to their need. God equates charity with faith. Those who do not share their wealth with the less privileged are idolaters. God is a friend of those who spend in charity in good times and bad.

Nations that do not establish social justice are doomed to extinction. They will be replaced by nations who are more charitably inclined towards the poor. Charity expiates some of your evils. Those who give in charity become pure. The charitable are truly religious.

Abundance is a gift of God. Seek it, but do not love wealth inordinately. Do not hoard wealth. Do not be stingy. Do not be extravagant lest you become reprehensible and destitute.

Please read this chapter in conjunction with Chapter 6 to find Qura'nic authority for what has been said. This will avoid repetition. However, I will quote some of the important verses on charity.

Righteousness is not that you should turn
Your faces to the East and to the West;
The righteous are those who believe in God and the last day
And the angels and the Book and the Messengers;
To spend of your substance out of love for Him, for your relatives,
The orphans, the poor, and the traveler.
For those who ask and to free the slaves and who pray regularly
and give zakat
And who fulfill their promises when they promise,
To be firm and patient in misfortune, affliction and hard times.
Such are the people of the truth, the God fearing. 2:177

And pray regularly and give zakat;
And whatever good you send for your souls, you will find with
God. 2:110p

They ask you how much they are to spend.
Say, "Whatever is beyond your needs."
Thus God clarifies the signs to you so that you may reflect. 2:219p

Those who give of their wealth, night and day, secretly and openly,
Have their reward with their Lord;
No fear will be on them, and they will not grieve. 2:274

Those who safeguard themselves against avarice
Those are the ones who thrive. 64:16p

Those who accumulate a hoard will face an agony that is inevitable.
70:18

And those in whose wealth is an acknowledged right
For the poor and the marginalized and those who stand by their
testimonies
They will be honored in the gardens. 70:24-25, 33, 35

Say, "O my God, possessor of all power-all good is in your hands
And You provide sustenance for whom You will, without measure."
3:26p-27p

Do you see the one who rejects religion?
This is the one who rebuffs the orphan
And is withholding neighborly assistance. 107:1-3, 7

Whatever God has awarded to the messenger of God
From the people of the cities is for God and the orphans
The destitute, and travelers in need
So that it won't circulate among the wealthy in your midst. 59:7

Those who are stingy and get people to be stingy
Hoarding what God has given them from the divine bounty
We have prepared a humiliating penalty for the atheists. 4:37

And do not keep your hand bound to your neck,
Nor yet stretch it as far as it extends,
Lest you become reprehensible and destitute. 17:29

You will know from the above verses that Islam favors free enterprise and heavy taxation to provide a strong social network for the underprivileged. Islam favors a social welfare state. If you look around for modern states following an economic system close to the Islamic economic system, then Canada, Sweden, Holland, and Norway are worthy of our attention.

Follow them and prosper.

Chapter Thirteen

GENESIS AND EVOLUTION OF MAN

God created man from water, from clay, from a single cell.   25:49 and 4:1p
Created in diverse stages.   71:14
From the posterity of other creatures. 6:133
Gave man the faculties of hearing, seeing, feeling, understanding and memory.
Taught him intelligent speech.   32:79p and 51:4p
Taught Adam the names of all things. 2:37p
Gifted him the faculty of inspiration.   2:37p
And finally breathed into man His spirit. 15:29

Chapter 13

Genesis and Evolution of Man

The **Qurán** propounds that evolution in the universe is a perpetual phenomenon. The nature around us is in flux, changing forms and evolving. Man similarly is subject to the same law of evolution and is slowly and imperceptibly being evolved. Life originated from water. Man was created from water, from clay. Man evolved from the posterity of other creatures, in diverse stages, travelling from stage to stage acquiring faculties of hearing, seeing, feeling, understanding and intelligent speech. Then Adam was bestowed with the faculty of choice-choosing from more than one option whenever available. And then Adam was gifted with the capacity to acquire knowledge-the names and nature and causes of all things. Then he acquired the gift of inspiration. And finally the Devine breathed into man His spirit. And the **Qurán** at this stage calls man 'Adam'. If man does not play the game according to rules he will be superseded by another form of life altogether new and unrecognizable to today's man. The Qura'nic verses in support of what has been said above are quoted below.

God is the creator of all things, the originator. 13:6 and **59:24**

God created the universe from a void. 6:101p

The heaven and the earth were joined together
Before We clove them asunder. 21:30

Creator of the heavens and the earth, who on having determined something,

Simply says to it, "Be" and it is. 2:117

And made all living things from water. 21:30p

And God has created every animal from water:
Of them are some that creep on their bellies:
Some that walk on two legs, and some that walk on four.
God created what He wills, for verily God has power over all things.
24:45

God created all things in proportion and measure. 54:49

This was the time when man was not worth mentioning. 76:1

God created man from water. 25:49

From an extract of earth 23:12

Created man from sounding clay 55:14

From a single cell 4:1p

God created all things in the best way and first fashioned man from clay
Then He made you in pairs and made your progeny from a sperm
drop.
Everything in man's life is recorded in a book. Paraphrased 32:7-9p
and 35:11p

And the Benevolent One has spread out the earth for His creatures.
Therein is fruit and date palms producing spathes
And grain with stalks for fodder and fragrant hops.
Now which of the blessings of your Lord will you deny?
55:10-13

Man was created from a single pair of male and female.
And made you into nations and tribes that you may know each other
And not despise each other. 49:13p

And gave man the faculties of hearing, seeing, feeling, and understanding.
And taught him intelligent speech. 32:79p,51:4p

Thus after a long period of evolution, a primate evolved into man.

God is self-sufficient and full of mercy.
If God willed He would remove you and replace you
With anyone God wishes, just as God created you
From the posterity of other creatures. 6:133

God has created you in diverse stages. 71:14

At this stage, man is called Adam by the **Qurán**. Adam is not an individual but the archetypal human. The first man, fully evolved and yet evolving.

Then God taught Adam the names of all things. 2:37p

And Adam learned from his Lord words of inspiration. 2:37p

Thus inspiration is another faculty which distinguished Adam from all other creations.

And breathed into him My spirit. 15:29p

Thus, every man and woman is also depository of a bit of divinity.

And We said: "Adam dwell in the garden but do not approach

This particular tree, lest you become wrongdoers." 2:35p

But Satan whispered evil to him.
Thus tempted, they both ate of the tree.
Thus Adam disobeyed his Lord and fell into error. 21:121p

Adam, exercising his newly bestowed gift to choose, made the wrong choice and fell. And Adam and Eve were banished to the earth. Nonetheless, **God made Adam the inheritor of the earth. 6:165p**

I will place a vice-jerent on earth. 2:30p

In this phase of life on earth God sent His messengers to guide mankind to take the right path, the straight path, the path of law. This point has been fully covered in Chapter 1.

You will surely travel from one stage to another. 84:19

It is man's destiny to travel until he meets his God, the Reality, the Light, the Law, and the Truth.

Forever toiling towards your Lord, painfully toiling,
But you shall meet Him. 84:6

Man has just started walking on the high road of knowledge and is accelerating towards his final destination, which is light years away.

And if all the trees on the earth were pens and the ocean were ink
With seven oceans behind it to add to its supply
Yet the words of God would not be exhausted in the writing. 3:12

Therefore patiently persevere and be in no haste. 46:35p

So incline your aim to religion,
To conform to the pattern on which God has made mankind.
There is no altering the creation of God, but most people do not know. 30:30

All affairs wind up with God. 42:53

The final goal is to your Lord. 53:42

Man at the same time is warned. If he falters in this process of slow and painful toiling, then:

We are not to be frustrated from changing your forms
And creating you in forms that you know not.
You already know the first creation,
So why not take a lesson. 56:60p, 61-62

Do not you see that God created the heavens and the earth in truth?
14:19

If God willed, He would remove you and bring a new generation. 4:133

God created you from clay, and decreed a second term (for you) And there is another determined term in the divine presence. 6:2p

God began the creation of man from clay And made his progeny from an extract of a lowly liquid Proportioned him and breathed some divine spirit into man Giving you hearing, seeing, intelligence. 32:7,8,9

If God willed, God would get rid of you And produce a new creation. 35:16

Hasn't there been a time when man was nothing worth mentioning? 76:1

It all adds up to the reality that from the time when man was nothing to the present day, he has gone through many stages of evolution and is yet active in this slow and imperceptible process. In the divine scale of time, man's life is only a blink of an eye. And yet we see ordinary men, extraordinary men, and super men amongst us. What will be his form in the final stage? The answer is deeply buried in the womb of Time.

Let us patiently persevere and be in no haste. 46:35 to conclude that you have reached the final stage, or you have understood God or His purposes.

Let me quote an interesting Qura'nic observation on man.

We offered the Trust to the heavens and the earth and the mountains. But they refused to bear it, being afraid.

But man took it up, for he is unjust and ignorant. 33:72

Chapter Fourteen

QURÁN AND ENVIRONMENT

Mischief has appeared on land and sea,
Because of the meed that the hands of man have earned.   30:41p

Man's mischief has disturbed the balance and proportion in
nature.   55:83p-67:3p

Those who corrupt the land are thieves. 12:73p

Do not do harm in the land as spoilers. 26:183p

Remember how God gave you a place to live on earth... do no evil
on earth by acting corruptly.
7:74

Do not obey the command of those
Who are extravagant, who corrupt the land
And do nothing to improve it. 26:151-152

Chapter 14

Qurán and the Changing Face
of the Environment

Muslims! Are you surprised that **Qurán** provides guidance to mankind on environment-an ultra-modern issue? Has any Muslim cleric researched the subject? How can he when these issues are outside his restricted and narrow ken?

Environment is the focus of man's attention for the past several decades. What is environment? In one sense which is relevant to this discussion, environment is the totality of things that surround us, conditions and factors and influences that impact life on earth-all life, be it visible or invisible, plant or animal, insect or human. The climate, soil, forests, rivers, rainfall, organisms and temperatures are all vital life-supporting components of the ecology. In them there is balance, order, ratio, proportion and equilibrium. If any of these are disturbed, whether caused by nature or man it may endanger life, disturb the food chain, and the availability of clean air and water. In the last fifty or so years, human activity has raised the global temperatures and caused what is popularly known as global warming. Industrialization, proliferation of mechanized land and air transport, use of refrigeration, microwaves, etc. are pumping hot and polluted air into the atmosphere. The rising temperatures have disturbed the natural equilibrium; resultantly, rainfall in some areas has increased and in some areas of the earth it has caused drought. Glaciers are melting, sea level is rising, tsunamis have gained strength and frequency, and coastlines and the communities living there are being threatened.

Man in his pursuit of affluence, in his greed, wastefulness and extravagance, has been consuming natural resources more rapidly than these can be replaced. Forests, minerals, seafood etc. are depleting. This is the gift of the developed countries.

Even the poor nations have contributed to the degradation of the environment. Increasing population with fixed resources like cultivable land and water and excessive cutting down of forests are threatening the very survival of the human race. Air and water, vital to life, are being polluted.

All this is contributing to poverty, disease, mischief on earth, and has led to disturbance in the equilibrium and proportion which God has established on earth.

Family planning in the developing countries is the crying need. This will restore the equilibrium around us, improve the quality of life, and avoid corruption on earth, where man is the vice-jerent of God. All this is in accordance with the Qura'nic injunctions.

In short, human activity has tipped this delicate balance, this ratio and order in our environment which has taken millions of years to establish. As far as we know so far, mother earth alone has produced this life-sustaining environment conducive to birth, sustenance, development, and evolution of life. All life on earth is man's kith and kin. Do not break ties with your kith and kin by acting mischievously. Man is god's vicejerent on earth, and the inheritor of the earth. It is his principle responsibility to nurture his abode, the mother earth.

Now the Qura'nic pronouncements on these vital, modern issues.

Mischief has appeared on land and sea
Because of the meed that the hands of men have earned,
That God may give them a taste of some of their deeds,
In order that they may turn back. 30:41

Do no mischief on the earth after it has been set in order.
Call on God with fear and longing. His mercy is always
Near those who do good. 7:56

Glorify the name of your guardian Lord who has created
And further given order and proportion
Who has ordained laws and granted guidance
Who has produced green pasture and made it brown waste

By degrees we shall teach you to declare the message
So that you shall not forget. 87:16

The sun and the moon revolve to a computation
And the trees and grasses bow down.
The Benevolent One has raised the sky and set the balance
So you would not overstep balance. 55:58

No want of proportion will you see in the creation
of God.   67:3p

Remember how God gave you a place to live on earth
So remember the benefit of God and do no evil on earth
By acting corruptly. 7:74p

Those who corrupt the land are thieves. 12:73p

People with balance and good sense should prohibit
Men from creating mischief on earth.
The wrongdoers pursue the excessive enjoyment of the good things
of life
And persist in sin. 11:16p paraphrased

Do not do harm in the land as spoilers. 26:183p
Do not obey the command of those who are extravagant,
Who corrupt the land and do nothing to improve it. 26:151-152

Is it to be expected of you that if you were put in authority
You will do mischief in the land and break your ties of kith and
kin? 47:22

Do no evil in the land. That is working mischief. 26:183p

Those who cut asunder things which God has commanded to
be joined are working mischief in the land-they are the cursed
ones.   13:25p paraphrased

We sent you not but as a mercy to all creatures. 21:107

Indeed, in the creation of the heavens and the earth,

And the alternations of the night and day
And the ships that sail the sea for the benefit of humanity,
And the water God enlivens the earth after its death,
And distributes all kinds of animals thereupon,
And the coursing of the winds, and the clouds employed
Between sky and earth.
Surely in them are signs for people who are wise. 2:164

There is a kind of person when empowered
He strives to do violence on earth,
Destroying the crops and livestock.
But God does not allow violence. 2:205p

Thus the message of the **Qurán** is loud and clear. All life is man's kith and kin. Do not disturb the delicate balance in our atmosphere. It goes to the extent of saying that you should not obey the command of those who are extravagant, corrupting the land, and are not doing anything to improve it. It is the responsibility of people with good sense and balance to prohibit men from corrupting the earth. The wrong-doers who pursue the excessive enjoyment of the good things of life are guilty of sin. Those who corrupt the land are thieves. If you disturb the equilibrium in the environment, mischief will appear on land and sea. Mankind is already tasting the bitter fruit of its deeds. It is time we turn back and restore the balance in nature. People in authority are expected to protect the land from mischief. If they fail, do not obey them, advises the **Qurán**.

Chapter Fifteen

CREATION OF THE UNIVERSES

Creator of the heavens from nothingness
Who on having determined something,
Simply says to it "Be" and it is. 2:117

Then God designed the sky which had been vapor. 41:11p

God created the heavens and the earth
And all between them in six eons. 32:4p

The secret of the heavens and the earth
Belongs to God and a decree of the end of time
Is as the blinking of an eye, even quicker. 16:77p

O humanity, be conscious of your Lord,
For the shock of the end of time
Will be a terrible thing. 22:1

The impending approaches-none can reveal it
But God. 53:57-58

Chapter 15

Creation of the Universes

Glorify the name of your Lord, the Highest
Who has created and given order and proportion
Who has ordained laws and granted guidance. 87:1,2,3

The **Qurán** propounds a theory of the creation of the universes and their ultimate fate.

The first universe was created out of nothing, out of a void which looked sort of vaporous. This creation came into being spontaneously, instantly, in the twinkling of an eye-in one command and a single order. The Benevolent One designed the first sky as a canopy with skill and power and constructed it with mathematical precision, spread the earth, and covered it richly to serve as an abode for man and to provide for his sustenance with things good and pure. The firmament was raised high and balance was established between the fundamental forces of nature. This balance is just right for all life to live and flourish and evolve. The Benevolent One warns man not to upset the balance, not to cause mischief on earth after it has been set in order, set in balance.

In the second stage, seven heavens and an equal number of earths were created in correspondence and in perfect harmony, in two eons. Each heaven was assigned its duty and command. Are you looking for flaws in God's creation, in the seven heavens? Keep looking. Look again and again; it will be a futile effort and your eyes will come back to you weak and weary.

The space is expanding and the process of creation of new universes continues. There is order, balance, and proportion in the creation of the

Divine, the self-subsisting, the uncaused cause of all that exists. Uncaused cause of existence, self-subsisting? This statement is significant and to get to its true meaning, one has to ponder hard and long. And be patient until man attains more knowledge and the ability to comprehend its meaning and significance.

A few significant observations on the creation of the universes are added.

The skies and the earth were one solid mass;
Then We split them. 21:30p

God did not create the heavens and the earth and everything in
between in jest; We created them for just ends,
But most of them do not know. 44:38-9

It is God who created for you all that is on the earth,
Then turned to the heights and fashioned themselves
Into seven heavens. 2:29

Creator of the heavens and the earth,
Who on having determined something,
Simply says to it: "Be!" and it is. 2:117

It is God who created the heavens and the earth
In six eons. 11:7p

Isn't the One who created the heavens and the earth
Able to create their like? Certainly, being themselves
Absolute creators, the omniscient one whose only
Command when willing a thing is to say to it: "Be!" and it is.
36:81-82

We have not created the heavens and the earth
And all that is between them,
But in due proportion and for a definite period. 46:3

God created the heavens and the earth with justice
That every soul be requited for what it earned,
Without being wronged. 45:22

God created the heavens and the earth by truth. 6:73p

The word of your Lord is fulfilled in truth and justice.
No one can change the words of God. 6:115p

When is the end of time set?

They ask you about the end of time, when is it set?
Say, "Only my Lord has knowledge of that."
And it will be knowledge of that.
It will only come to you suddenly as a surprise." 7:187p

God alone has the knowledge of the end of time. 31:34

Now the Qura'nic authority for what has been stated:

God is the creator of all things. 13:6

God is self-subsisting.
Wherever you turn, you encounter God. 3:2p

This is God, the creator, the originator. 59:24

It is God Who created the heavens and the earth by truth,
The day God says "Be" then it is. 6:73

Isn't the One who created the heavens and the earth,
Able to create their like?
Certainly, being the absolute Creator. 36:81

It is God who created for you all that is on earth,
Then turned to the firmaments
And proportioned them into seven heavens. 2:29

God has created the heavens and the earth in just proportion
And formed you, fashioned you expertly
And the destination is to God. 64:3

Do not you see that God
Created the heavens and earth in truth?

We did not create the heavens and the earth
And everything between them in jest;
We created them for just ends
But most of them do not know. 14:49 and 44:38-9

God created the heavens and the earth with justice,
That every soul be requited for what it earned,
Without being wronged. 45:22

Creator of the heavens from nothingness,
Who on having determined something
Simply says to it "Be" and it is. 2:117 and 40:68

Then God designed the sky which had been vapor. 41:11p

We have not created the heavens and the earth
And all that is between them
But in due proportion and for a definite term. 46:3p

We have created pairs of everything
So that you may contemplate. 51:49

God is the One who created seven heavens
And as many earths, with the order
Descending among them. 65:12p

God created the seven heavens in correspondence;
You see no disharmony in the creation of the Most Gracious.
Now look: Do you see any flaw?
Turn your vision again and again.
Your gaze comes back dazed and weary. 6:7

Glorify the name of the Guardian Lord, the Highest,
Who has created and given order and proportion,
Who has ordained laws and granted guidance. 87:1-3

God created the sun, the moon, and stars
Subject to the divine order. 7:54p

Everything in the heavens and the earth glorifies God

The First and the Last, the Outward and the Inward. 57:2-3

Every day He shines in new splendor. 55:29

**God created the heavens and the earth
And all between them in six eons. 32:4p**

**Everything in the heavens and everything on the earth Glorifies God.
His is the sovereignty and His is the praise. 64:1**

The Last Hour-When the Universe is destroyed, when time stops.

As there was a beginning of the universe, there is an end to it. The end of the universe is also the end of time. Hence time and universe are coeval. The last day will dawn with the sounding of a trumpet once and calamity takes over. On this day the dealers in falsehood will lose out, the sky will be like a molten brass, humanity will be scattered like moths and the mountains like carded wool.

The sun is rolled up, the stars fall lusterless, the oceans are flooded, the blaze is flared up. In short, the universe will have collapsed into itself and reverted to the state before it was born, a void, a nothingness.

**They ask you about the end of time,
When it is set?
Say, "Its end is up to your Lord." 79:42, 44**

**All upon earth perishes, but the face of God endures forever,
Majestic, Sublime, and Giving. 55:26**

**We created the heavens and the earth
And everything in between them for justice
And since the end of time is sure to come,
Then forgive human faults with gracious forgiveness. 15:85**

**We have prepared a blazing fire for those
Who deny the end of time. 25:11p**

On the day that time stops. 40:46p

And when the last hour dawns. 30:55p

So expect a day when on which
The sky will produce a visible smoke or mist
Overwhelming the people. 44:10, 11p

To God belongs the dominion of the heavens and the earth, And
the day on which the end of time will happen, a day on which the
dealers in falsehood will lose out. 45:27

The impending approaches-none can reveal it but God. 53:57-58

The day the quake will convulse and another will follow. 79:67

When the sun is rolled up, when the stars fall lusterless
When the mountains are blown away,
When the oceans are flooded,
When the blaze is flared up,
When the garden is drawn near,
Each soul will know what it has brought about.   81:1,2,3,6,11-14

What is the catastrophe?
A date when humanity will be like scattered moths
And the mountains like carded wool. 101:3,4,5

Do they feel sure that the end of time
Will not come upon them unawares, suddenly? 12:107p

The secret of the heavens and the earth belongs to God
And a decree of the end of time is as the blinking of an eye,
Or even quicker. 16:77p

O Humanity, be conscious of your Lord,
For the shock of the end of time will be a terrible thing. 22:1

The unbelievers say, "The end of time will never come upon us."
Say, "Oh yes, by my Lord it will surely come upon you."
All this is recorded in the manifest Book. 34:3p

It is God Who has the knowledge of the end of time. 31:34p

All affairs wind up with God. 42:53p

**The sun and the moon
Follow courses exactly compounded. 55:5**

**Neither can the sun overtake the moon
Nor the night outpace the day.
Each swims along in its orbit according to law. 36:40**

You will find no change in Our Law. 17:77

None can challenge the Word of God. 6:115

Important Note

Let me state what the latest scientific conclusions are. Stephen Hawking and Leonard Mlodinow in their book THE GREAT DESIGN-New Answers to the Ultimate Question of Life have come up with what they call the M-Theory. "The M-Theory may offer answers to the question of creation. According to M-Theory, ours is not the only universe. Instead M-theory predicts that a great many universes were created out of nothing." Let me quote what the **Qurán** has to state on this.

**God created the <u>heavens </u>and the earth
With justice. 45:22**

**Isn't the One who created the <u>heavens </u>and the earth
Able to create their like? Certainly, being the
Absolute creator. 36:81**

Creator of the <u>heavens</u> from nothingness 2:117p

God designed the sky which has been vapor 41:11p

The grand design further states: "The creation of the universes does not require the intervention of some supernatural being or god. Rather these multiple universes arise naturally from physical law. They are a prediction of science."

Islamic God defines himself in innumerable ways. I quote only two of them which are relevant here.

God is the uncaused cause of all beings 112:2
Reference-THE MESSAGE OF THE QURA'N by Mohammad Assad

They have not truly assessed the measure of God.
God is transcendent beyond any association they make. 39:67p

Could the "uncaused cause of all beings" be the supernatural being or god, a creation from the physical law? We will have to wait a little more before human knowledge is able to unravel this mystery.

Chapter Sixteen

FREE WILL VERSUS DETERMINISM

Insights from your Lord have already come to you; so if anyone sees, it is for his own benefit. And if anyone is blind, it is to his own detriment. And I am not a guardian to watch over you. 6:104
So whoever accepts guidance does so to the benefit of his own soul and whoever strays only strays to the detriment of his own soul. And you are not the one to dispose of their affairs. 39:41p
On the day of resurrection the wrongdoers will be told: "Taste what you have earned." 39:24p

Chapter 16

Islam and Free Will Versus Determinism

The debate whether man inherently enjoys the freedom to act and behave as he likes or whether his destiny is determined by forces external to himself has been going on since the early classical period. And its resolution is nowhere in sight. But the grand **Qurán** settled this issue long ago.

Islam is firmly on the side of the free will. In all of life forms, man alone has been vouchsaved free will, the ability to choose between different courses available to him.

Qurán is a book of guidance for all mankind-a touchstone to distinguish between right and wrong, between good and evil. It restricts itself to defining the right path-the path that ensures man's salvation in this world and the next. Man is left free to go the way of his choosing, thus assuming full responsibility for his choice and the consequences that flow from it. This is true of individuals, societies, tribes, nations, or civilizations. And the path that leads to prosperity or adversity in this world and the next has been identified in the **Qurán** and all other scriptures in their original forms, the forms as revealed to the prophets. The societies, the nations, the tribes, the individual humans, will meet their meed in this world. Human history is littered with fallen civilizations. The divine exhorts man to walk about the world to see the debris of past civilizations, to study the causes of their downfall, and avoid such blunders to ensure that the existing civilizations travel linearly. All this has been brought out in Chapters 1, 4, and 11. Man is solely responsible for the rise and fall of civilizations and the divine does not interfere in this process. In Christianity man's destiny is pre-ordained, and he has no part in the unfolding of the drama in which he plays the lead role. The unfolding is in accordance with God's grand design. Jesus Christ who has been conferred the divine status by the church, has by his death on the cross ensured the redemption of his followers. As a consequence, the doors of hell are closed on them. This philosophy appeared to have appealed to early Muslim theologians who adopted this position, suitably modified for Muslims. They have taken the position that the Prophet of Islam intercedes with God on the day of judgment on behalf of his followers and God forgives them all, thus booking a berth in heaven for Muslims.

This is contrary to the Quranic stance. (For details please see Chapter 2.) Man has been granted the gift of free will. His destiny is tied to his conduct. Pre-ordination knocks out the pedestal on which morality stands, from which all religions, faiths, and creeds draw strength and sustenance. The entire structure of reward and punishment becomes redundant. Evil is not punished and the good receive no reward. If all stand on equal footing, where is the need for hell and heaven? (Please see details in Chapter 2.)

Man is God's vicejerent, the inheritor of the earth, the bearer of the divine spirit. Man's superior knowledge, his capacity to learn, and freedom to act independently, a choice which has been denied to the angels, places man above the angels. God therefore orders angels to fall in obeisance to the human. Is it conceivable that man, the vicejerent of God on earth, the inheritor of the earth and a being superior to angels and a proud bearer of the Divine spirit within himself, could be a silent spectator, a helpless creature, a slave to his destiny? This is most unlikely. Let me state the observation of Stephen Hawking and Leonard Mlodinow in their book THE GRAND DESIGN: "Each universe has many possible histories and many possible states at later times, that is, at times like the present, long after their creation. Most of these states will be quite unlike the universe we observe and quite unsuitable for the existence of any form of life. Only a very few would allow creatures like us to exist. Does our presence select out from this vast array only those universes that are compatible with our existence? Although we are puny and insignificant on the scale of the cosmos, this makes us, in a sense, the lords of creation." page 9, 2010 edition. Man is in command of his destiny and charts out the path on which he treads. He suffers if he chooses the wrong path, but prospers in this world and the next if he makes the right choice. According to the Quranic philosophy, man is a free agent and has the freedom to act out his own destiny. So are nations. Adam had the freedom to disregard God's advice and suffered the consequences.

Now the Quranic authority for what has been stated above.

A book of guidance for mankind.
Sent by divine grace with Truth.
Guides mankind to ways of peace and safety.
To a path that is straight. 5:115

Book of Guidance, a guide to mankind 2:2, 3:4

A Book of Guidance, a criterion between right and wrong 2:185p
and many others

Haven't they traveled the earth and seen
How those before them ended up?
They were more powerful than these,
And they plowed the land and populated it,
And their messengers came to them
With indisputable evidence.
It was not God who wronged them,
But they wronged themselves. 30:9

Then the end of those who did evil
Will be the worst, as they repudiated
The signs of God, and used to deride them. 30:10

If you did good, you did good for yourselves;
And if you did wrong, it was to yourselves. 17:7p

For We have sent you the Book
For mankind, according to truth.
So whoever accepts guidance does so
To the benefit of his own soul,

And whoever strays only strays
To the detriment of his own soul.
And you (Muhammad) are not the one
To dispose of their affairs. 39:41

Insights from your Lord have already come to you;
So if anyone sees, it is for his own benefit.
And if anyone is blind,
It is to his own detriment.
And I am not a guardian to watch over you. 6:104

God does not compel a soul
To do what is beyond its ability:
One gets what one has earned
And is responsible for what one deserves. 2:286p

Those who cut asunder things which God has commanded to be joined
Are working mischief in the land.
They are the cursed ones. 13:25 paraphrased

Mischief has appeared on land and sea
Because of the meed that the hands of men have earned 30:41p

Do no mischief on the earth after it has been set in order. 7:56p

Do not do harm in the land as spoilers. 26:183p

I will place a vicejerent on earth. 2:30p

God made Adam the inheritor of the earth. 6:165p

And breathed into him My spirit. 15:29p

And We said: "Adam, dwell in the garden,
You and your wife,
But do not approach this particular tree,
Lest you become wrongdoers." 2:35p

Then Satan made the two slip from there,

**And caused them to depart
From the state they were in. 2:36p**

**If you reject God, He has no need of you...
No bearer of burdens can bear the burden of another.
To your Lord is the return.
You will then be told what all you did. 39:7p**

**On the day of judgment, the wrongdoers will be told:
"Taste the fruit of what you have earned." 39:24p**

**As for those who scoff
And repudiate Our signs,
They are inmates of hellfire,
Wherein they remain." 2:39**

Do we notice Divine intervention in human affairs anywhere?

All his life, the Prophet of Islam operated within the constraints of natural laws. No miracles were vouchsaved to him.

(For full details, see Chapter 3.)

In conclusion, I would like to reiterate that the **Qurán** is an eternal book of guidance for all of mankind. Only the learned, the highly learned, the wise and those who think, ponder, and contemplate standing, sitting, walking, and lying down on their sides on God's creations, are capable of fully understanding the Book. At any given time, the interpretation and understanding of the **Qurán** is tentative-linked to the depth and the state of man's knowledge. The meaning evolves and gains significance with increase in knowledge. God of Islam is universal. His laws are immutable and apply to all. All are equal before Him. All this has been brought out fully in the chapters on **Qurán**, Divinity, Muhammad (PBUH) and Knowledge.

The image explained

The image on the book cover depicts the spectacular sunrise in the desert of Arabia, signifying at the same time the dawn of Islam. The night, the heavens and the heavenly bodies in the image are frequently mentioned in the **Qurán**.

The cube-shaped image reflects the cube-shaped Kabah-the sacred house of God in Mecca, the spiritual focal point of Muslims. Kabah was originally built by Prophet Abraham and his son, Prophet Ishmael, in the distant past to commemorate the name of God, the one God forever. Later generations, however, turned it into a sanctuary of idols, placed by their followers. It is said that an image of Jesus Christ also adorned this gallery of deities. Today's Kabah is a simple stone structure fifteen meters high, twelve meters long and ten and a half meters wide.

When Mecca was subdued by the Muslims in 630 CE, the prophet of Islam ordered clearing of idols from the Kabah, and restoring it to its pristine, monotheistic status. (The inside now is bare and empty.) It is said that the prophet recited the following verse continually when the idols were being removed. **The truth has come and falsehood has perished because falsehood is bound to perish. 17:81**

About the Author

Syed Zahoor Ahmad was born on May 4, 1934, in Bangalore, India, and belongs to a family of Qazis (Islamic judges). He migrated to Pakistan with his family in the April of 1948. He holds two master's degrees in English literature and economics from Pakistan and a master of science degree in transport studies from the University of Leeds, England. He is widely read. History, philosophy, and religions are his special areas of interest. He has a deep understanding of the **Qurán**. Mr. Ahmad now is Pakistani American and lives in Ocala, Florida, with his wife and has four children.